Embracing the Darkness:

How a Jewish, Sixties, Berkeley Radical Learned to Live with Depression, God's Way!

By

Daniel Mann

[handwritten: From Novia, to Ana, Blessings in Christ! Daniel Mann 2007]

Introduction

> "[God] …comforts us in all our affliction so that we may be able to comfort those who are in any affliction with the comfort with which we ourselves are comforted by God," **(2 Cor. 1:4)**.

Depression had been nipping at my heals for as far back as I could remember. Sometimes, due to alienation at school and anti-Semitism, it had me in its bear hug. I didn't have a clue about countering it. The various therapies, religions, and lifestyles I resorted to proved little better than quicksand. The more I struggled, the deeper I sank.

I tried to outrun it. In 1970, I left the USA to roam around Europe and the Middle East, always on the move, sleeping in barn and field, anywhere I could find relief.

In 1976, I came to a final way-station that promised ultimate relief, the Messiah. I had an initial "honeymoon" period. I saw and experienced things I couldn't deny. Nevertheless, depression again blindsided me with another unwelcome visitor, panic attacks. The faith that I thought would weather the storm ran away terrified. The God that I had thought I had come to know, if He indeed existed, didn't respond to my flimsy and desperate cries for help. Perhaps He did exist, but He just didn't like me enough. In any event, I found myself devastated for the next several years.

I continued to pray and to seek God for answers, not because I believed that He would eventually answer me but because I had no other place to turn. I had tried everything else! I didn't really trust God anymore, but I trusted Him more than anything else.

I was convinced that if Christianity was the truth and Christ died for my sins, I shouldn't be feeling the way I was. If He loved me, He would answer my prayers. There was no reason why I should be more dysfunctional and suicidal than those who didn't even have a faith in Christ. Surely, my experience had to disqualify Christianity, but Christ remained my only hope.

I now look back over my years of suffering in a way I never thought I'd be able. I never thought I'd be able to honestly thank God for the pain. However, it's been through the pain and utter despair that He's taught me so much. I'm reminded of Paul's cry of anguish: "Indeed, we had the sentence of death within ourselves in order that we should not trust in ourselves, but in God who raises the dead," (2 Cor. 1:9). Through the ordeal, my Savior has indeed become dear to me in a way that couldn't have been otherwise. It's through the ordeal that I've come to love Him as He is and to even accept myself despite my many imperfections. My weaknesses serve as a token of His undying love. They remind me of the extent of His love and tender care of this life.

He has provided richly for me through my suffering, especially through what He has taught me. That's what this book is about. Paul commented frequently about how this is a necessary process. The only way we can truly be of comfort to others is through the comfort God has given us in the midst of our own suffering.

This book started as a course I've been teaching at the New York School of the Bible entitled, "Biblical Principles for Handling Depression and Despair." It then became a seminar which I now bring to prisons and churches.

I feel so blessed to be privileged to present God's life-transforming truths, especially as I see animation and even excitement overcoming discouraged faces. I've also been so encouraged by their verbal responses. One prisoner wrote, "This seminar beats any anti-depressant I've ever had." One pastor wrote that he had been thinking of giving up both life and ministry before attending the seminar. Of late, I've been finding that depression has become a precious key allowing me an intimate entry into other lives.

I don't claim to be the recipient of a hidden strategy or method of treatment. Rather, I'm just passing on what God has given me, His wisdom that is available to all through Scripture, but even more so, Himself! It's the wisdom that enables a proper faith-relationship with Him.

The book is divided into two major sections. The first deals with the content of the seminar along with additional autobiographical material which illuminates my many embarrassing missteps. The final several chapters critique secular counseling. An addendum provides additional autobiographical material for those so interested.

Contents

In the midst of depression it's hard to even hear the Word. We need to know that our growth and recovery are in God's hands, not in ours. He delights in reversing hopeless situations, namely our weaknesses, faults, sins, and despairs. He even uses them to accomplish great things.

With a purely materialistic philosophy, secular clinical practice and theory adversely impact counseling. Secularism can't consistently impart respect, meaning, and hope. However, these concepts rightly belong to Christianity. Christianity provides the necessary perspective and Person to cope with suffering.

Before a new structure can be built, the old one must be removed. The same principle pertains to the Christian. The old belief system has to be purged away lest it infiltrate and corrupt the new. Suffering places pressure upon the old system until it gives way.

Trusting in our own righteousness is antithetical to trusting in God's righteousness. It's also impossible to achieve and will psychologically kill us. However, it's very difficult to convince others of its presence and of its dangers.

We are being transformed into the image of whatever it is that we admire and worship. When we sin and try to justify ourselves, we turn from light to darkness. This in turn banishes us from the healing light of God. We can't adore God while we are trying to justify self. The two are mutually exclusive. One results in negative transformation, the other in positive.

We were made to serve and to fear God. From this we derive our worth. To our detriment, we instead serve to gain the good favor of others. While this will degrade us, serving God ennobles.

Having inflated expectations can lead to disappointment; having diminished expectations can lead to inactivity. Christianity navigates a course of sanity between Buddhist detachment and hedonistic attachment. Life is good and many aspects of it are to be affirmed, but our ultimate fulfillment is to be found in the next world.

When we worry about whether or not we have enough faith, we take our trusting focus from God and place it upon ourselves. Faith isn't a matter of quantity or even primarily a matter of quality but of focus. If we are trusting in God rather than in ourselves or some other thing or agent, we can reassure ourselves that we have "enough" faith.

Seeing and accepting ourselves as we truly are is a pre-condition for psychological integration, wisdom and peace. Many recognize that the pursuit of a higher self-esteem is inimical to this and that we have to step outside the "performance cycle." We can only achieve true self-acceptance if our identity is based upon something more solid than our performance. Only God is solid enough.

Accepting only the "idealized self" (IS) is antithetical to any intimate relationship. Scripture has an answer to this profound danger: Biblical standards are impossibly high. We're either humbled by our failures to meet these standards or we reinterpret Scripture to agree with our delusions of self-righteousness.

Without this we can't trust in God as we aught and become vulnerable to despair. The answer consists of recognizing that it's natural to experience inner turmoil and weak faith and that this doesn't preclude God's love. Assurance is ultimately based upon the presence of faith itself but we also derive comfort from our behavioral response to faith.

We're promised love, joy, and peace, but all too often we don't see these fruits and despair. In order not to despair, we need a model to understand God's workings. This model demonstrates how God uses law, obedience, failure, repentance and grace to produce His own very special fruit. Seeing how it all works together brings reassurance.

Part 2: Christianity and Secular Therapy

Trying to recover repressed memories to relieve inner conflict often proves unfruitful for numerous reasons. Memories may be unreliable. Furthermore, there are reasons why we repress. These underlying reasons must be meaningfully dealt with before we can confront what's been repressed. Psychoanalysis erroneously assumes that we're willing and able to deal with this material. The answer is not to build self-esteem to counteract guilt and shame, but to deal with them objectively through confession and accepting God's forgiveness.

Although self-awareness is important, many pursue it in all the wrong places and ways, namely, in trying to understand how we became the way we are. There are several problems with this pursuit. It's tenuous, unfruitful, it tends to impart a negative perspective, it divides, and leads us away from more fruitful areas of self-awareness. The Christian alternative depends upon faith and repentance.

Behavioral Therapy succeeds only if the clients believe that they have achieved mastery over their fears or problems. However, this victory can be very tenuous. If their newfound confidence is a product of the belief that they now can successfully confront the controlling problem, new experiences can deprive them of this confidence. Self is an inadequate foundation for confidence.

Although there are many areas of agreement, Cognitive philosophy erroneously equates depression with irrationality. Experimentation shows otherwise. Instead, the depressed need hope in the midst of their pain and failure. If this hope is placed upon the self, it further burdens an already overburdened psyche.

The application of principles alone will not get us to where we want to go. This can't happen apart from a daily relationship with the Living Savior.

Part 1

CHRISTIANITY

AND

DEPRESSION & DESPAIR

CHAPTER 1

A Biblical Orientation Toward Suffering & Depression

> If God is for us, who can be against us? He who did not spare His own Son, but delivered Him up for us all, how shall He not with Him also freely give us all things? **Romans 8:31-32**

This verse joyously trumpets the fact that it's not about us but about God. It's not about our strengths, skills, or any aspect of our performance; it's about a God who intends to shower us with blessing. It's not about our clawing, climbing, or earning our way into His presence; it's about a Redeemer who reached down into the lowest slime pit to draw to Himself those who despised Him. This gives us license to say "goodbye" to past failures and rejections, inabilities and the sense of unworthiness. It beckons us to turn away from inadequacies and the scars of past insults, injuries, and childhood traumas. Truly, if the master of this entire universe is lending His muscle to our lives, what need we fear?

Nor does He leave us dangling over the precipice of our fears of failure and rejection. He's bought us; we belong to Him and amazingly, we're "in Him."[1] This means that our self-image is who He is; our significance is matter of this Redeemer's own worth. Against our every perception otherwise, we're told that we are clothed with the righteousness of God Himself.

However, we often find that we can't even lift our head high enough to drink in the comfort of these assurances. Years of defeat, despair, and depression have shriveled our expectations and hopes so that our palate rejects such food.

I suspect that this had been Moses' experience after 40 years in the desert. Forty years earlier, he had put God first, identifying with His slave people, Israel, rather than the comforts of Egypt and his royal privileges. He was going to lead Israel to freedom. Moses gambled and lost everything. He was rejected by the very people he sought to liberate. Having no other recourse at this point, he fled to the wilderness empty handed. At the end of the forty years, God appeared to him in a burning bush to offer him the very mission Moses had so enthusiastically undertaken 40 years prior.

However, this time around, it was different. Moses declined the appointment claiming that he lacked the ability. His humiliation and despair had probably been too crushing. In response, God tried to reassure him that it wasn't about Moses' ability but God's,[2] but Moses wasn't buying any of it.[3]

It's difficult to hear the words of the Lord after years of defeat and depression. For so many years, I watched as I saw my personal defects bringing about one failure after another, heightening my sense of isolation, alienation, and shame. As hard as I would struggle against my sins and defects, employing all the prescribed spiritual disciplines, the more bitter and depressed I became. I was struggling against quicksand. The more I struggled, the deeper I sank. On top of everything else, I was now a failure and had to cope with the accompanying shame of being an inveterate failure. I'd resent others who'd experienced success in overcoming the types of things that continued to rub my face in the mud.

THE SAILBOAT ANALOGY

A friend residing in Maine took Anita and me for a ride in his sailboat. The wind was with us, and it carried us to the far end of the lake. I thought that we'd have to wait for the wind to change in order to return. To my great surprise, I found that it didn't matter from what direction the wind was blowing. Our friend was able to harness the wind and to use its energy to carry the boat in whatever direction we wanted. He might have to zigzag a bit to get there, but getting there wasn't a problem. The important thing was that there was a wind. Without any wind, we wouldn't be able to move.

The same thing is true about the "winds of our life." God can harness these winds to take us in any direction He so chooses. Our weaknesses and inadequacies constitute no problem for Him. He isn't limited as we are. He can mold us into anything that He wants as a potter can mold his clay into any shape he so desires.

This was the very thing that was so hard for me to see. I suffered daily from childhood-induced trauma. I didn't see any redemptive good in any of it. Because of this perspective, life looked bleak indeed. It was a place of pain and despair. I thoroughly subscribed to the secular understanding of the day: pain equals defeat and shame, while happiness is equated with success, friendship, and attractiveness. I was on a downward spiral—the more shame, the worse my performance, the worse my performance, the more shame.

It would be a mistake to close our eyes to how childhood influences cause suffering. It's part of our lives and it exerts a profound affect upon all our thinking and doing. Nevertheless, we need not be trapped within this perspective. There's a greater perspective that comes into view as we turn from the temporal and look to the Divine where we see God harnessing these "winds" or afflictions to create a beautiful mosaic out of our lives.

Sometimes, He beckons us to merely watch. "Be still, and know that I *am* God; I will be exalted among the nations, I will be exalted in the earth!"[4] Sometimes we're called upon to be proactive in the assurance that He is leading the way.[5]

Moses had taken a big hit. We don't know what his perspective had been. Had he been blaming himself? Perhaps there had been some deficiency in his coddled existence in the courts of Egypt that had led him to make such an unwise gamble, one that left him destitute? How could he have made such a wrong assessment about those ungrateful Israelites? Perhaps it was some insecurity that had prevented him from being content with his lot at Pharaoh's court, which made him seek his sense of significance through a higher moral calling? What was the matter with him that he couldn't find satisfaction in the things in which others found satisfaction?

From our mountain top perspective, we can see that such musings, although they might contain some truth, miss the point of the greater narrative. Whatever the causes, Moses was suffering, but it wasn't for naught. He had been adopted by Pharaoh's daughter and had been groomed for power.[6] His forty years in the desert hadn't been a relaxing vacation. We get this impression from the name he assigned to his firstborn, "Gershom," meaning, "I have become an alien in a foreign land." He had to eat "humble oats," but this experience was a hurricane harnessed by God to produce great humility in Moses,[7] a trait that would later serve him well.

God uses every wind, weakness, and infirmity to create a glorious story. He's promised to work all things together to accomplish His loving plan for our lives.[8] As ashamed as I have been about my weaknesses and brokenness and as much as I have wanted to be thoroughly rid of them, I also know that God uses all my afflictions for good purposes. Fear can be one of the most difficult things to live with. It can totally entrap us within a virtual nightmare. However, God has used fear, in this lazy man's life, to make me more careful, to exercise more forethought, and to prepare better-crafted lessons for my students. Teachers have to be very concerned about what they say. I enjoy the creative part of writing and putting together lessons, while I detest and avoid the corrections and the rewrites. However, the fear of failure and humiliation prevent me from taking the easy way out and "shooting from the hip."

Anger can so powerfully take command of our thinking and distort our perceptions. Anger had often convinced me of the righteousness of my cause when I wasn't right at all. It had also led me to do foolish and costly things, even at an early age. At the tender age of six, returning home from school with all sorts of pent up discomfort, I strained to open our heavy from door, which was on a spring. It slipped out of my hand and sprang back upon my thumb, resting within the doorframe. I screamed in pain. However, instead of removing my thumb, in anger at my unpardonable mistake, I again pulled the door back and this time intentionally slammed it upon my thumb. Through tears and anger, I repeated this process until my nail fell off.

Self-punishment isn't a good outlet for anger. However, anger does serve useful purposes. Jesus became angry and allowed that anger to express itself in a righteous way.[9] Perhaps you've known people who don't experience much anger. Have you noticed that they ignore problems that should be addressed and that these problems have a way of growing?

God can use anything that we bring to Him. He used Moses' humble shepherd's staff to bring mighty judgments upon the nation of Egypt. How much more can He use those emotions that He had instilled within us! He can even make use of our depression and despair to bring us to the spiritual, intellectual place of His choice. Moses had despaired of himself. He didn't think himself able to fill the shoes God had set before him. Had Moses thought that He was adequate for the task, he would have fallen. He wouldn't have had the dependence upon God that made his ministry possible.

Depression can kill, but in God's hand, it has a way of reordering our priorities, stripping from us everything that we had thought we needed, to show us that only one thing is important.[10] This is something noted by even Buddhist psychotherapists. They see depression as an opportunity to escape our old mindset, to get out of the rut of physical existence. However, their goal is very different. For them the answer is to come to an awareness of "oneness," that reality is one, that we are all one, and that distinctions are illusion.

Jealousy even has its appropriate arena. We are told that God is a jealous God. He is so concerned about His people that He doesn't want anything to negatively impact their welfare. God can also redirect our jealousy so that it too might become a wellspring for love.

Let me anticipate your challenge: "That's fine for God's jealousy or perhaps someone else's jealousy, but my reactions aren't very pretty. There's nothing redeemable about them."

GOD CAN HARNESS ANY WIND

Jeremiah lived in a tumultuous time of impeding destruction. Continually, he had the unenviable task of carrying a message of "doom and gloom" to his people and experienced unceasing heartache as a result. On top of this, he had to tell them that it was their entire fault. God told Jeremiah to inform them,

> " 'Because your fathers have forsaken Me,' says the Lord; 'they have walked after other gods and have served them and worshiped them, and have forsaken Me and not kept My law. And you have done worse than your fathers, for behold, each one follows the dictates of his own evil heart, so that no one listens to Me. Therefore I will cast you out of this land...' "[11]

It seemed to Jeremiah that there was no hope left for either himself or for Israel. God told him to go observe a potter and how the potter was able to do whatever he wanted with the clay. God then gave Jeremiah the interpretation: God could also mold His people into models of trust and obedience.[12]

Our Master Potter is also molding us according to His master plan. He made us just the way He wanted and even determined the length[13] and even the details of our lives.[14] To accomplish this, our Potter doesn't require our strength, our spiritual successes, or even our health and wholeness. In fact, He prefers it when we're utterly weak and sick[15] so that we wouldn't be tempted to take credit for His workmanship.

God had commissioned Gideon, a very ordinary man, to militarily rescue Israel from her oppressors. However, it had to be done God's way.

> "And the Lord said to Gideon, 'The people who *are* with you *are* too many for Me to give the Midianites into their hands, lest Israel claim glory for itself against Me, saying, 'My own hand has saved me.' ' "[16]

God eventually whittled down Gideon's 22,000 man army to a mere 300 to make it plain that it wasn't about their valor, but about God alone. He wanted them to understand that the victory would be His alone.

If we were truly able to embrace this truth in every corner of our being, we wouldn't feel so ashamed of our brokenness and weaknesses. Instead, our most shameful parts become doorways into glory. How much more do we come to esteem God's righteousness when we see the utter inadequacy of our own! God's forgiveness in view of our own unworthiness! Paul came to understand that if he was going to rejoice in anything, it'd have to be his brokenness and weaknesses because they are God's glorious materials, not our successes and giftedness.

THE EXAMPLE OF MARTIN LUTHER

Much has been written about the great saints of the Church from a psychological perspective. Martin Luther has been analyzed with microscopic scrutiny. I've found some of the results quite interesting and perhaps revealing of the struggles of this giant of the faith. However, if these pebbles are investigated apart from the enormous edifice they've served to build, they loose all their significance. They only find their meaning as a part of the greater structure. It would be like trying to enjoy reading <u>Brothers Karamazov</u> by trying to enjoy each word in isolation of the rest. Any word only assumes its full meaning in context. Without context, there can be no meaning.

From all indications, Martin Luther, the great reformer, emerged from the confines of his family carrying a crippling assortment of battle scars. His father was overbearing and highly critical of young Martin. There was nothing he could do to please this tyrant of a father of whom he lived in fear.

As a young man, he finally escaped the clutches of his father to devote his life to the service of God as an Augustinian monk. But even there, his wounds festered. He writes,

"When I was a monk I thought that I was utterly cast away, if at any time I felt any evil motion, fleshly lust, wrath, or envy against any brother. I went to confession daily, but it profited me not...I could not rest but was continually vexed with these thoughts: 'This or that sin thou hast committed; thou art infested with envy,...and other such sins; therefore, thou art entered into this holy order in vain.'"[17]

He perceived that his infirmities had rendered him unfit for godly service. Even worse, he had been presumptuous to think that he was spiritual enough for the Augustinian order and now his presumption was apparent to all.

Elsewhere, Luther wrote about the Vicar of his order, Johann Von Staupitz, to whose confessional he continually resorted hours each day. Not knowing how to counsel Luther in a way that would alleviate his inner turmoil, he finally told Luther to just love God and to not worry about the rest. To this Luther exploded, "Love God? I hate him!" Luther had a father whom he could not please. Now he served a God who had even higher standards! How would Luther please Him? He was driven to utter despair.

In a very real sense, Luther's scars made him unfit, unfit to counsel others, to teach, even unfit to praise God. Fortunately, Luther had only one place to turn in his desperation. He writes,

"Although an impeccable monk, I stood before God as a sinner troubled in conscience, and I had no confidence that my merit would satisfy Him...Day and night I pondered until I saw the connection between the justice of God and the statement, 'The just shall live by his faith.' Then I grasped that the justice of God is the righteousness by which, through grace and sheer mercy, God justifies us through faith. Therefore, I felt myself reborn and to have gone through open doors into paradise. The whole of Scripture took on a new meaning and whereas before, the 'justice of God' had filled me with hate, now it became to me inexpressively sweet...This passage of

Paul became to me a gate to heaven."[18]

Luther's scars, rather than rendering him unfit for service, had led him to rediscover for the Church it's most precious yet most easily corrupted truth—"salvation by grace through faith alone." What had caused Luther great suffering and bondage led to his ultimate liberation? Had Luther been more successful at the impossible task of trying to earn God's favor, he would have contentedly remained an Augustinian monk and the advent of Protestantism, with its message of grace, might have had to await the coming of another broken and tormented soul, unable to find comfort in a "good works" theology of salvation.

Ironically, it seems to have been his infirmity that most qualified Luther to fulfill his ordained task of rediscovering the depths of God's grace. Who more wholeheartedly would have rejoiced in God's forgiveness than a man so consigned under His wrath.[19]

Indeed, we can, in some regards, understand Luther's life from the perspective of past influences. However, if our understanding stops there, we miss the big picture, the real narrative. The real narrative begins with a plan and a dream. The plan is God's—to redeem a people and to prepare them for an unimaginable eternal glory. The dream is ours—to find ultimate love and significance. However, this dream has become marred, and we grope blindly trying to fulfill it in all the wrong places. In the course of this groping, we suffer and despair of the dream. Meanwhile, Destiny is fulfilling it in greater ways than our dream can fathom. In the next chapters, I'll discuss the role that depression and despair play in His plan.

EXERCISE

1. How do you feel about your suffering, weaknesses, and afflictions?

2. Do you now see how they might have some redemptive significance? How?

3. Seeing that they do have a redemptive significance, does that change your feelings towards them? How?

4. How might you encourage others based upon these insights?

---

[1] 2 Corinthians 5:21
[2] Exodus 3:11-4:13
[3] Exodus 4:14
[4] Psalm 46:10
[5] Phil. 2:12
[6] Acts 7:22
[7] Numbers 12:3
[8] Romans 8:28
[9] John 2:17
[10] Luke 10:42
[11] Jeremiah 16:11-13
[12] Jer. 18:6
[13] Psalm 139:15-16
[14] Matthew 10:30
[15] 2 Corinthians 12:9-10
[16] Judges 7:2
[17] Commentary on Galatians, Martin Luther
[18] Ibid.
[19] This had been Luther's experience of God.

CHAPTER 2

Conceptualizing Suffering & Depression

> "No temptation (ordeal) has overtaken you but such as is common to man; but God is faithful, who will not allow you to be tempted beyond what you're able to bear, but will with the temptation make a way of escape, that you may be able to bear it." **(1 Cor. 10:13)**

Are you mentally ill, deranged, or just an inadequate personality type? Is the pain you experience an abnormality, a product of an unhealthy childhood? Or are you a sinner, and is your pain to potential path to reconciliation with the Light?

How we understand suffering and mental health issues is key to the answers we seek and ultimately find and even how we feel about ourselves. Few of us have been left untouched by the insights of Western, secular psychotherapy. These insights have permeated our thinking to such a large extent that we see the world through its lens. We need to understand how this lens colors our vision and also to see how the lens of Biblical understanding gives us an alternative vision.

Secular clinical practice and philosophy fail to provide an adequate basis for respect, hope, and an appreciation of the meaning and depth of human experience. It's out-of-step with human reality. People struggling with depression and other life-controlling problems struggle with guilt and shame. Therefore, the therapeutic setting has to provide respect. The therapist has to also be able to see beyond the failure and illness of the client and to convey a vision of hope. However, these are the very things that secularism can't provide if it's going to be true to its own colors.

To understand this, we have to see what secularism is. Secularism either represents a denial of a transcendental reality or spirituality or their neglect. This means that "what you see is what you get." Reality is reduced to what can be felt, seen or touched. Consequently, the secularist has no philosophical basis to believe in the essential value or sanctity of all human life. The distinctions among people are glaring. Some are beautiful, others ugly; some are lovable, others not; some are productive, others a financial drain; some are moral and valued by society, others a detriment; some are considered mentally ill, others not. Lacking a transcendent perspective, the secularist is necessarily bound by philosophical materialism to dictate what she perceives about her client. Admittedly, often what we see is not very pleasant nor respectable. However, for the secularist, there is no other dimension from which she can draw. Philosophically, there is no basis for respect if the client is not respectable.

Nevertheless, the client must be affirmed and respected, but the way the client is actually regarded is very different. This leads to schizoid practice. While the secularist explicitly practices "unconditional positive regard" and superficially conveys respect, something else is implicitly being conveyed. If all you see is what you get, then there are vast differences in worth among people. How much worth can a terminally diseased man have if he is comatose and will die tomorrow? It could even be argued that he has a negative worth upon his family and society. He is a liability. Yet we all know that we can't treat people solely based upon their temporal value, especially if we want to enter into a healing relationship with them.

What then must the secularist do? Bite the bullet! Although she knows that she has to treat her dysfunctional client in a way that suggests that the client is just as worthy as others, the secularist belief system doesn't cooperate. One way to live with the inconsistency is to merely tell yourself, "Life is filled with inconsistencies. We just have to learn to live with them and to go with what works." When truth and pragmatism collide, pragmatism generally wins out. Pragmatism gives the immediate rewards, but with the diminution of truth comes the diminution of substance and meaning. But what are the *long-range* results of such a "victory?" Where practice collides with theory, one of them will eventually give way.[1]

Christian revelation provides a perspective that allows us to see others through a majestic lens. We were created in His image,[2] which means that we all possess a worth that transcends our circumstances, performance, and appearance. Even the infirm and the rejected possess a worth that's eternal. This is a lens through which respect and hope are clearly perceived. This is a respect and a hope that aren't manufactured for the situation to manipulate the client into wellness. The hope is a real hope, one that looks beyond the pain and failure of our mangled lives into the nurturing embrace of our first Parent.

The Christian perspective allows us to confront the fact that we're all "sick." None of us are good, according Paul.[3] We're all infected with the same virus that contorts both mind and body into rheumatoid lumps. It involves both cognitive and affective dysfunction. Christian revelation starts with the assertion that we're all created in the image of God, but we weren't satisfied. We rejected intimacy with a divine Being in favor of autonomy, truth in favor of immediate gratification. In order to deny the primacy of truth and the desperate cries of the conscience, we've had to resort to self-justification, the willful distortion of our mental processes to enable us to see what we wanted to see and to avoid the obvious. We came to hate the light and love the darkness.[4]

Although it had been hard to see things this way, I eventually found this message liberating. Yes, I was a "loser," as I always knew I was, but everyone else was also a "loser." I no longer had to be ashamed around others. Admittedly, the Bible paints a bleak portrait of human beings, but we can find great solace in this portrait if we already have an inkling of its truth. It gives us permission to stop running and hiding, to stop putting on our front. It allows us to relax and to accept ourselves, the compromised person that we always knew was us, and to say "goodbye" to the exhausting preoccupation with image management.

I always get a uniformly positive response from my classes when I say, "There are only two types of people—the jerks and those who don't know that they're jerks." Everyone giggles knowingly. They now see themselves as jerks, as their own worse enemy. However, there was a time when everyone else, apart from themselves, was a jerk.

We might be sick or jerks, but we've been commissioned to serve within a drama, the most central and meaningful drama of all human history, serving the greatest Force, the Source of all truth and love. In this drama, it doesn't matter what our limitations are. In our weakness and sickness, we're made strong by our King who is able to compensate for any of our failings. Nor do we need be concerned about what others might think of us. Truly, they may see us as valueless or degraded, but there is only one opinion that matters. Paul assured the Roman church that they shouldn't be concerned about the opinions of others. No one could bring a charge against God's people.[5] Any basis for a legitimate charge had long been removed. Only God's opinion mattered.[6]

It's okay to be broken or sick. A Christian can say this, mean it and have reasons for it. For the secularist, sickness is the opposite of health and ultimately of value and significance. It has no redeeming value. It's to be avoided as a plague. Seeing the larger narrative, the Christian can affirm pain.

DEPRESSION DOESN'T MEAN THAT SOMETHING HAS GONE WRONG.

Jeremiah, the Prophet who had been called from the womb, had stated, "My grief is beyond healing, my heart is broken."[7] He had been called to be God's right-hand man. Although it is truly ennobling to directly serve the ultimate source of all love, truth, and power, Jeremiah also found this calling to be extremely painful, so much so, that he cursed the day he was born and had cursed those who had brought the message of his birth. God's call doesn't mean instant happiness. Instead, we're promised that the road to glory is a painful one.

King David is known as the man "after God's own heart." However, this didn't result in favorable treatment. David had to suffer all the more because of it. Favored status has its costs. In despair, David cried, "O Lord, how long will you forget me? Forever? How long will you look the other way? How long must I struggle with anguish in my soul, with sorrow in my heart every day?"[8] Depression is more than normal. It's the mud with which God makes His building bricks.

Some might protest that David needlessly suffered because of his sins, and if we would not sin, we would not have to suffer. Indeed, sometimes we do bring needless suffering upon ourselves because of our sin. The same David had written, "I am on the verge of collapse facing constant pain. But I confess my sins; I am deeply sorry for what I have done."[9] Clearly, David recognized that his suffering in this instance was the result of sin, but is all suffering the result of sin or our defects? Certainly not!

Jesus had suffered as much as anyone but not because of His own sin. "Filled with anguish and deep distress," Jesus took three of His disciples with Him to pray. He confided, "My soul is crushed with grief to the point of death. Stay here and watch (pray) with Me."[10] Sometimes no amount of faith or confidence in the future can stem the pain. We're human beings. Pain goes with the turf.

Anita once coaxed me, with bribes of head-rubs, to ride the roller coaster with her. I was assured that I'd exit this amusement ride alive, but while I was on it, I screamed for my life. My horror wasn't the result in any deficiency in faith but a reflection of the fact that I have another nature that was screaming "bloody murder."

Sometimes we punish ourselves with the thought that, "I should be doing better or at least responding with less upset. After all I have learned and experienced, I can't understand why this problem is getting me down."

In the midst of His suffering in the Garden, an angel came and strengthened Jesus. Certainly, after such supernatural ministrations, Jesus would have been able to proceed without such anguish. Instead, afterwards, the account reads, "He prayed more fervently, and He was in such agony of spirit that His sweat fell to the ground like great drops of blood."[11] Jesus knew better than to reprimand Himself for not feeling more relieved after the angelic visit.

We too often respond as secularists, failing to see the hand of God. However, the more that we realize that this experience of suffering, depression, and despair is normal,[12] the quicker we can cease punishing ourselves and accept our experience as part of a divine plan. In conjunction with this, it's so important to understand how this suffering is accomplishing great things in God's hand.

SUFFERING AS A HEALING TOOL

God inflicted Paul with blindness, striking him down from his horse during his venture to persecute the followers of Jesus. Meanwhile, God was informing a follower named Ananias to go to lay his hands upon Paul so that Paul would regain his sight. Ananias protested that Paul was the man who was killing Christians, but God reassured him, "Go, for he is a chosen vessel of Mine to bear My Name before Gentiles, kings, and the children of Israel. For I will show him how many things he must suffer for My Name's sake."[13]

Preparation for divine service demands suffering! Paul would not be able to serve God faithfully without this preparation. No pain, no gain. First, Paul had to see that he had been blind. Physical blindness might have reflected the fact that he was also spiritually blind. Suffering then reorients our vision from the darkness of complacency to light.

Serving God means trusting Him fully. However, we can't trust God until we learn to not trust in self. Insofar as we trust in self, we fail to trust in God. The two are mutually exclusive![14] Here's the rub—our entire sense of security rests upon our confidence that we can handle life's problems. Living without this sense of security is utterly painful and disorienting, but it has to go in order to make room for God. How can we pray to God with any earnestness while believing that if God doesn't come through, we can handle it just fine on our own? Instead, when we come to see God as our only hope, prayer becomes a lifeline.

Paul writes about going through such trials that he "despaired even of life." We have this erroneous idea that if we are living right, good things should happen. Fortunately for Paul, he didn't share this fiction. He accepted his experience knowing that there was a reason for it. Suffering and failure didn't destroy his hope but resurrected it. He writes, "We had the sentence of death in ourselves so that we should no longer trust in ourselves but in God who raises the dead."[15] Christianity doesn't deny that there's a lot wrong with us. It acknowledges that the malady is also the cure, and that despair can be liberating. Under the scalpel of God, the disease is His manure to grow roses. What had brought shame has now become the seedbed for strength and beauty.

UNDERSTANDING THAT GOD IS IN PERFECT CONTROL PRODUCES PEACE AND HOPE.

God is the perfect craftsman. He can use the most unlikely circumstances to produce His desired effect in our life. It is so easy to believe that our decisions, mistakes, or sins can take us outside of the parameters of God's love and power. We become certain that we've blown it and fall into despair. This is why God has to reassure us that not only is He able to work all of our circumstances in accordance with His divine plan for our lives, but this is what He actually does. If we know this, we can even rejoice when it hurts.

"...We also glory in tribulations, knowing that tribu-
lation produces perseverance, and perseverance character;
and character, hope. Now hope does not disappoint,
because the love of God has been poured out in our hearts
by the Holy Spirit..."[16]

Everyone recognizes the need for hope and meaning. Without
these, we can barely get out of bed in the morning. Even Friedrich
Nietzsche, the avowed enemy of Christianity, pointed out that "He
who has a 'why' to live for can bear almost any 'how.'" Christ
provides the ultimate "why"—eternal glory with God in heaven!
What was Nietzsche's "why?" —a "freedom" that culminated in his
insanity, a "power" that ended with death. Nietzsche's belief system
was incapable of producing hope. He denied the existence of any
purpose outside of ourselves. There was no higher Truth to which we
could aspire. We were completely free to create our own reality, but
that put all of life's challenges and pains upon our own back. There
would be no supernatural rescue, no Power to give meaning and hope
within the context of pain. What is the "why" of secularism? —a
vague, undefined concept of health that no one ever realizes.

Victor Frankl wrote about his experience in a Nazi death
camp.

"The prisoner who had lost his faith in the future—his
future—was doomed. With his loss of belief in the future,
he also lost his spiritual hold; he let himself decline and
become subject to mental and physical decay."[17]

Although many of us have experiences that have born out the
truth of this observation, it's difficult to manufacture meaning
where we have none. Frankl recommended that the inmates establish their own "why" by determining to find their loved ones after
this ordeal or by becoming a living witness to the horrors of the
death camp. As worthy as this "why" might be, many of us confront
such unspeakable horrors of our own "death camps" that only a
God-infused "why" could possibly suffice.

Secularism can't provide hope. It just adds to the burden. If we only go around once, and if life isn't enjoyed to the fullest, then we've lost out. A life of sorrow and depression can have little redeeming value even if we recognize that we learn and acquire sensitivity and empathy through it. It all ends with our last breath. Although many secular therapists would like to inject meaning into the sinews of human experience, even into the painful ones, they find themselves blocked by their philosophy. Consequently, many have gravitated toward a Buddhist philosophy, which affirms the existence in an afterlife, albeit an impersonal one. Equipped with this understanding, they can affirm that depression is an opportunity to learn and thereby to escape from the illusions of this material world.

> Arthur Deikman, a psychotherapist with a strong Buddhist orientation writes,

> "Human being needs meaning. Without it they suffer boredom, depression, and despair…Western psychotherapy is hard put to meet human beings' need for meaning, for it attempts to understand clinical phenomena in a framework based on scientific materialism in which the meaning is arbitrary and purpose non-existent. Consequently, Western psychotherapy interprets the search for meaning as a function of childlike dependency wishes and fears of helplessness…"[18]

For Western psychotherapy there is only pathology and the lack thereof. It has no "why." It merely encourages the client to find his own meaning, while suspecting that this is just another manifestation of his pathology. There's nothing to affirm. Everything is flat. There is no honor, integrity, or courage; there's just self-interest.

For instance, we might still be touched to see DiCaprio sacrifice himself for his beloved in the movie "The Titanic." However, if we are to react consistent with our secularism, we need to reprimand ourselves for such a reaction. "What a jerk! DiCaprio experiences chemicals secreted into his inter-synaptic cleft and neurons firing. He likes those feelings and he kills himself because of these chemically induced feelings. He stupidly believed that there was something more than chemistry going on, that his feelings represented more than the chance movement of chemicals but some higher truth, and this foolishness killed him." At best, we find ourselves stretched between two very different responses. We are moved emotionally, but our minds say, "baloney!"

We can't divorce the way we feel from the way we believe. When I was 19, I embraced a secular ideology and proclaimed my complete freedom from any "truth" or higher reality. When I saw someone give a couple of dollars to a street urchin, I scorned the giver. I felt that there was something so insincere about it. He wasn't giving the money because of some higher truth, which didn't exist, but because it enabled him to feel valuable. The act of giving convinced him that he was a good person. As such, he used the urchin for his own selfish purposes. If everything was selfish and self-centered, and I was convinced that it was, it represented a greater "truth" to be openly self-gratifying than to play sanctimonious games by superficially helping others.

However, this philosophy didn't accord with human nature and proved to be unlivable. By rejecting my natural human instincts of friendliness and service in favor of the life I wished to create for myself, life rejected me, and I slid deeper into the jaws of depression. Nihilism proved to be dehumanizing, depriving me of the God-given appreciation of the depth and meaning of human experience and of any non-self-centered concept and experience of love, honor, integrity, and self-sacrifice.

Our lives have to count for something. We are more than just sensory creatures, craving new and more exciting feelings. We also have mind and conscience, and these must be wholistically coordinated with our feelings if we are to find peace. I've often seen movies that had fantastic acting, sets, and special effects, and although my feelings were highly stimulated as I watched, at the end I was left very dissatisfied. I might have found it morally offensive or intellectually unsatisfying, non-illuminating and poorly crafted. My teenage nephew informed me that he loved "The

Matrix" because it opened up a new and fresh way of seeing things. He found it *intellectually* satisfying and placed it #1 on his list. We can't profitably divorce ourselves from the perspective of meaning and truth. David Karp, a sociologist who himself has battled the ravages of depression, writes in <u>Speaking of Sadness,</u>

> "We're built to seek significance, a significance and a purpose that transcends experience and feelings alone. Secularism tells us that there is no moral truth or ultimate meaning out there. We have to invent it' and this we do according to our needs or psychological script. Therefore, there is nothing out there to seek. It's just a matter of determining your needs and fulfilling them."

For life to have meaning and purpose, Karp recognizes that experiences must be more than mere experiences. They have to serve a greater purpose. Even those things that we esteem least, our hurts and brokenness, need to be invested with a higher significance if we are to accept our unseemly failings. It's not enough for us that our stories are a chance, chaotic collections of unintegrated events. They have to be vital parts of a grand, defining story, but such a story requires a divine Story-Teller. There's no way around this.

I've recently noticed that many of the themes of popular movies include providential elements. An improbable hero is meant to lead the rebellion to save mankind and, unbeknownst to him, nothing can stop him, although the forces of evil are desperately trying to do so. Why is this concept of "inevitability" so appealing, and how can we seriously embrace it without also embracing a Being who makes our story inevitable? We want to believe that there's a controlling power, but scurry for the dark when it becomes evident that this Power must be a personal and righteous God. We can't have it both ways. If we opt in favor of meaning and truth, we've opted for a *found* truth, not one we've created, but for a God who created that found truth.

However, even if brokenness serves some eternal purpose, it's not enough to know this. We continue to fumble through life, making wrong decisions and finding that we lack what it takes to take advantage of the lessons that pain might teach. I was convinced that if left to my own to change or to learn certain lessons, I'd fail. There might be an eternal purpose, but I would fail to grasp hold of it and to appropriate it successfully into my life. I just didn't have what it took to connect with God.

While I lived in Israel for two years starting in 1970, I began to search for God, at least in my own way. I asked questions of everyone who professed to have a religion. I used to torment friends and acquaintances with my questions about God. Finally one annoyed friend told me that she couldn't answer my questions, but that the Lubavitchers could. They are a Hasidic sect with centers both in Crown Heights, Brooklyn and Lod, Israel. They welcome Jewish people who are searching.

The next day, I was knocking on the door of Kfar Chabbad, their headquarters where they had a Yeshiva, their seminary. The Rabbi immediately found me a bed at the Yeshiva dormitory. There were three beds to a room, and I was informed that luckily one had just been vacated. I readily agreed to go along with the program that included study and religious practice. It was like feeding corn to a hungry pig. Even their daily ritual of stomping through the halls while banging on a pot to wake up the students I found acceptable.

Many of the others there were like me. They too were young American Jews who had come to Israel searching for something. However, unlike myself, they appeared to have found what they were looking for, so much so that they talked with a Yiddish accent and gestured like Jews from Poland. However, I was impressed with their fervor. Instead of talking about where they had been what they had done, they were consumed with Talmud and living the Jewish life. They smoked like chimneys and yelled like Met fans, but it was all about Talmud. Although I couldn't understand what made them tick, I was among my own. I no longer had to feel like the ugly duckling. Here were others, Jews, who had the same concerns as I had. At least they didn't look at me as if I was crazy when I asked my questions.

"How do you know God exists?...Who is He?...How does He affect your life?" I queried. I stayed up late asking my questions.

Although I found many who were willing to give me an answer, I had a hard time processing the answers and was often left unsatisfied. One evening, an American came up to me.

"Danny, I know exactly what you're going through. That's because a year ago I was going through the exact same thing as you are now." I was all ears.

"There is a Tzaddik in Tel Aviv who can open up the Torah for you and prove to you beyond any shadow of doubt that the Torah is God's Word!" Many Jews believe that there are only 49 Tzaddiks in the whole world at any one time, and that it's their prayers that hold the world together. They were intermediaries between God and us. I was excited. This was exactly what I was looking for! I would have one very important piece in the puzzle.

David made the arrangements, and the next evening we were aboard a bus heading for Tel Aviv. I was surprised at myself. My heart was beating as if I was going to my own wedding. This was an evening that might change my life.

We wandered through the back streets of Tel Aviv, David leading the way as I panted along behind him. We climbed the stairs of the backside of a building in an alleyway. Surprisingly, it opened into a great hall filled with black attired Hasidim excitedly milling around waiting for their Rabbi, the Tzaddik, to emerge. Evidently, David had been here numerous times before. He informed one of the Hasidim of our arrival and of our appointment with the Tzaddik. We were informed that as soon as the Tzaddik was ready for me, we would be informed.

Meanwhile, the Hasidim (the faithful) were making ready the table for a feast. Every meal with their Tzaddik was a feast. He was God's representative among them and everything they did reflected this fact. He would commence the bread and the wine, and they would have the privilege of eating after him. Everything that the Tzaddik did revealed heaven's wisdom, and none of it was lost upon the Hasidim. I watched their preparations spellbound as my heart entered into their own excitement.

Finally, a Hasid came and informed me that the Master was ready and led me back to see him. The Tzaddik sat at a narrow table and silently motioned me to sit down across from him as he studied me intently. The silence continued for some time as he continued to study me. My excitement grew. With his long beard and deep sunken eyes, the Tzaddik had a profound otherworldly appearance. He wasn't embarrassed to stare at me. He was well beyond such considerations, and I comforted myself with the knowledge that I was in the presence of a real Master. Not only would I have the answers that I was looking for, but I would also have a personalized answer.

I watched him, not wanting to do anything to interrupt his concentration. However, as I continued my vigil, he began to shake his head from side to side. This unexpected gesture disturbed my reverie.

"You're not ready," he informed me shrugging his shoulders.

"Excuse me," I responded trying to maintain my composure.

"You're not ready," he repeated. "Ready for what?" I thought, fearing the worst. I was at heaven's gate, and it seemed as if I was being told that I couldn't enter.

"You're not ready to study Torah," he added. "There's too much tension in your life," waving his hairy hand in the air as if to dispel the tension. My heart sank. I knew that he was right, but I also knew that there was little I could do about it. I had tried many times. Who wants tension anyway? I had hoped that maybe, if there was a God, God could do something about that, but according to the Tzaddik, I had to get my act together before God could help me. I was the ugly duckling, a leper, cast away from the gates of Eden and condemned like Cain to wander endlessly.

"You need to go to a Jewish Kibbutz and live the Jewish life and then come back in a few months and we'll talk again." It sounded like the end of the interview. I was worth less than a minute of his time. I didn't even get a chance to ask one of my questions, and I was being dismissed and sent out into the outer darkness. I knew that his Kibbutz recommendation wouldn't work. I had already spent a lot of time on several Kibbutzim, and I was as tense now as the day I had started.

"You have the impertinence to not even hear a single word from me, and you're passing judgment upon me! You aren't even as smart as you think you are. If you were, you might have anticipated this outburst of mine and handled the situation differently," I thundered.

Even though I thought that he was absolutely correct in his assessment of me, I felt so hurt, I vomited forth my desperate cry in the only way I could. Nevertheless, this didn't change the verdict, the verdict that I had believed for years, the verdict that he had merely confirmed. If there was a God, I certainly lacked what it required to get to Him. A God who was there to merely help me wasn't God enough. I needed a God who would jump into my brokenness, take me by the hand, and lead me all the way. He had to do it. I couldn't.

ACCEPTING BROKENNESS

We all have a self-concept. We continue to scrutinize self and others to obsessively readjust this concept. When we perform well, we tend to feel worthy of love and secure within ourselves. When we don't perform well or aren't popular or lack whatever it is that our performance expectations might consist, we feel unworthy, unlovable, and uncomfortable around others.

I needed to be convinced of two things. I needed to know that there was a greater power than myself, a Power who could make up for all my deficiencies, a Power who could cradle me in His arms and take care of my every need and failing. I also had to know that this Power would not be turned off by my constant failure to meet performance expectations.

We also tend to project our personal standards upon God. If we aren't performing to the level of good works that we have deemed adequate or have determined that we're not spiritual enough, we become convinced that God doesn't love us, or at least doesn't love us enough. As our performance improves, we suppose that we become more beloved by God, and as it falls, we become very uncomfortable with our relationship with God and may even begin to resent Him for holding us to such an unobtainable standard.

I imported my self-mortifying performance standards into my newfound faith. As long as I was meeting my standards, everything was OK. However, God loves us too much to leave us with our self-righteousness, which constitutes a denial of the sufficiency of

His righteousness.

The more that my own righteousness deteriorated in my own eyes, the more desperate I became to prop it up. I began to make "visits of mercy" to the elderly at nursing homes and the infirm at hospitals. I assured myself that God would be happy with this and that I'd be able to "earn" my way back into His graces. However, a labor of fear isn't a joyous one. I wasn't visiting out of love for the residents but rather an oppressive fear of the consequences. It was a job, and they were merely objects I was using to earn relief from fear.

I'm sure that the objects of my mercy marveled at my appearance. I didn't display any of the signs of love and concern, which characterize people who devote themselves to this type of ministry. Instead, fear and great discomfort oozed from my pores. They were clearly enduring my visit, patiently awaiting the length of time I'd have to spend with a patient before I'd feel justified to flee to the next.

Self-righteousness kills. It represents the failure to accept brokenness, the truth about ourselves and the all-surpassing reality of grace. It's a denial of God's righteousness in favor of our own performance and the sense of superiority it offers. More people have died at the hands of those who felt that they were self-righteously entitled to subjugate others because they had attained to some exalted level of righteousness than from all the combined forms of criminality. Christians who have fallen prey to "salvation by guilt-induced charity" flee from this distortion in several different ways. Some join "Christians Anonymous;" others reinterpret the Bible in such a way to relieve their guilt: "God doesn't expect us to be 'goody-two-shoes'." Both solutions fail to address the problem of our deeply ingrained self-righteousness.

Recovery is a three-step process. We have to recognize that God calls us to the same standard of righteousness that He lives by. Second, we have to despair of attaining this righteousness through our own performance. Lastly, we have to see that God loves us in spite of our failures, especially in our despair and brokenness. We call this faith.

BROKENNESS IS BEAUTIFUL

For God, brokenness is beautiful. This is so counter-intuitive but so clearly true. Isaiah surprises us with these words: "I dwell on high and holy place with him who has a contrite (broken) and humble spirit, to revive the spirit of the humble, and to revive the heart of the contrite ones."[19] Isaiah is speaking about those who are so crushed by life that they need to be "revived." He is speaking to the loser, the failure, to the ones who know they don't have what it takes even to follow God, to those on the point of despairing, even of God. This is so unexpected. The verses that assert that those who sow will reap and that God blesses those who are faithful tend to resonate with us.

Shouldn't those who are performing well be the ones that are experiencing a greater closeness with God? However, Isaiah insists, "But on this one will I look: on him who is poor (in spirit) and of a contrite spirit, who trembles at My Word."[20] Isaiah is not alone in this message. The Psalms continually echo the same hope to the broken and despairing. Jesus reiterates this same theme in the Sermon on the Mount, proclaiming the blessedness of the "poor in spirit" apart from any achievements on their part.[21] This is a perplexing message on several accounts. What's to become of the "contrite" after they become more assured of God's mercy and no longer need "revived?" It's unthinkable that God would lose interest in us once we become more assured of His love and begin to crawl out of our hole. Similarly, how do we reconcile the assertions that God blesses the faithful and the counter-assertions that God blesses the broken and struggling? How can His blessings extend to both groups?

Once we experience brokenness (perhaps for long stretches of time) and come to receive the mercy of God, we come to realize through this mercy, even as we grow in faithfulness, we remain "broken" and utterly dependent upon God. We may no longer experience clinical depression, but we come to know that all good things come from God and that the moment we flatter ourselves into believing that we can succeed without God, we set ourselves up for a giant fall.[22] We also come to see that whatever good we find in our lives is a gift from God, and therefore, we're in no position to look down upon anyone. We stand by the mercy of God alone. In this we come to affirm without hesitation our poverty in spirit even as we live faithfully.

This might sound depressing, but it is such a blessing to be able to live comfortably with this "poverty." If I can truly accept this brokenness, I can accept everything else about myself. If I can accept the painful, I can also accept the comfortable. I can drop all pretence, all image management, the endless labors of trying to impress others, and the burden of trying to be someone else. It's so liberating to find that we can laugh at ourselves, even about those things that had brought us intense shame.

All of this is made possible because the God of the universe is willing and desirous of loving us at our worst, even to the point of dying for us while we were His enemies.[23] Paul reasons from this that if God loved us so much then, at the cost of His own intense suffering, how much more now!

This is brought home very poignantly to me when I consider others who unknowingly spoke a hurtful word against me. Although I seldom sought revenge, I found that I'd positively delight myself in their misfortunes. How uncharacteristic is this of our suffering God who continues to lovingly pursue His enemies.

WHY BROKENNESS IS SO PRECIOUS TO GOD

Why must we go through life-choking suffering? Why can't He be pleased by something a little easier to endure? Are we to be pleased as we look upon the suffering of others?

The tears of brokenness serve as a prism through which we can begin to see the light of God. Any meaningful relationship must rest upon a foundation of truth. I learned this the hard way. When I was 14, I established my own religion with myself as god. The dividends were excellent, at least at first. I would stand in front of my mirror and perform sacred worship, telling myself how well I looked. (I used to have a much better build.) Even more than that,

I'd convince myself that I was better than others in just about every respect and that I could handle anything that life threw at me. These devotional speeches worked for a while, giving me a sense of superiority and confidence. However, I wasn't able to take account of the enormous price I was paying for the privilege of being god.

As with any drug, I was receiving diminished returns for my investment. As time went on, I found that I couldn't obtain the buzz of the initial "highs." Desperately, I searched for a more potent fix. The fix had to be potent enough to set me back upon the throne I had established for myself. I found that I could also achieve a small high by putting others down. At least, comparatively, I could still achieve some semblance of god-ship. However, I had condemned myself to a life of obsessive comparisons between myself and others.

It's hard to be god. Along with the glory come certain responsibilities. I had to prove to myself that I rightfully deserved my office. I then needed the fix of god-like performances and successes, at least a level of performance that exceeded that of others. I had to hit a home run each time at bat and was unable to accept failure when everything within me was so craving the confirmation of my worth. It shouldn't be any surprise that with such personal requirements, I resented those who succeeded where I failed.

Friendship was a very fleeting luxury. It is said that two people can't walk together unless they are agreed. My life repeatedly bore out the wisdom of this statement. The way we see ourselves must coincide with the way others see us if we are to enjoy a harmonious relationship. I think we subtly emit messages about ourselves that are either affirmed or negated. When negated, we experience dissonance and isolation. Unknown to myself at the time, I was "demanding" that others see me as I saw myself with my grossly inflated self-estimation.

It is possible to find others who will "worship" us, at least for starters. But eventually, reality sets in, and my newfound friends became increasingly unwilling to grant me the higher status I so craved. Of course, there were never any *explicit* demands, but eventually our hearts' demands impress themselves uncomfortably upon our relationships.

If the parties can't agree, an uncomfortable feeling of distance results. Anita had just finished painting our apartment. She had labored mightily and had done a magnificent job and understandably wanted to hear expressions of my appreciation. I did appreciate what she had done, but my feelings were more mixed than hers. It was a long and painful experience for me. It had disrupted my life, and that had been my primary concern, and I wanted her to appreciate all the discomfort I had experienced. While I wanted to give her the affirmation that she desired, I didn't feel that I could honestly affirm her work to the extent she wanted. We had a series of uncomfortable negotiations until we fortunately arrived at a common understanding.

A meaningful friendship with God must also be built upon mutual understandings of whom we are and whom God is. Self-righteousness is a denial of the necessary common ground for a relationship. The religious leadership held a very different set of definitions than did Jesus. Luke grants us a telling account of their dissonant exchanges.

> "The Pharisees, who were lovers of money,....derided Him. And He said to them, 'You are those who justify yourselves before men, but God knows your hearts. For what is highly esteemed among men is an abomination in the sight of God'."[24]

The Pharisees were "esteemed among men." Their delusions were socially shared. Others also believed that they were truly superior human beings and conferred that respect upon them. This made their delusions especially resistant to change. Nevertheless, somewhere in the marrow of their bones they knew the truth about themselves and vainly tired to justify themselves and to reassure one another in the face of Jesus' charges against them, charges that would eventually lead Jesus to the Cross.

Their attitudes were an "abomination in the sight of God." It wasn't that the Pharisees were worse sinners than everyone else. In fact, in terms of the external performance of the requirements of

God's Law, they out-shined all the rest. When Jesus would cast doubts about their relationship with God, His own disciples were startled. If the Pharisees weren't saved, who then could be!

Instead, the Pharisaic problem was one of the heart. Their self-concept and God-concept were an offense to God, and they hardened themselves in their self-righteous attitudes as Jesus pounded upon their doors. They refused to wake up, smell the coffee and repent. Jesus didn't love them any less than He did the others despite His harsh words against them. These harsh words were words of love. Later, while looking over Jerusalem, He exclaimed His hearts desire to make them His own children, but they continually refused.[25]

Had Jesus instead showered His blessings upon them while they were in their hardened state, He would have *enabled* them to remain with their delusions. Had I found friends who would have been willing to consistently shower me with praise and respect, I would have become hardened in my delusions and would have become more resistant to change. Why change if my lifestyle is paying me healthy dividends?

In contrast to the Pharisees, Jesus painted us a portrait of the type of character He was very ready to bless and embrace.

> "Then Jesus called a little child to Him, set him in the midst of them, and said, 'Assuredly, I say to you, unless you are converted and become as little children, you will by no means enter the kingdom of heaven. Therefore, whoever humbles himself as this little child is the greatest in the kingdom of heaven.'"[26]

For the Jewish people of Jesus' day, this was a radical message. Little children hadn't yet accrued any merit before God. They were takers, not givers, but in their favor, they knew that they didn't deserve anything. They knew that the good that they received was merely because someone loved them. They therefore were without any pretensions that they deserved anything from God. God could gladly bless them without any concern of enabling them to believe in their own self-righteousness or deservedness.

Relationship must be based upon truth. To put it plainly, the truth about humanity isn't pretty. Just look at the way we crucified the Son of God and all the other prophets of God. As far as we know, all of the Apostles died a martyr's horrible death. Look at the incessant warfare, greed, xenophobia, and self-centeredness. It's hubris to think that we're any different. God requires that intimacy must be predicated upon a true accounting of who we are and who He is. Before all else, repentance and confession is a process of coming to terms not only with God but also with ourselves.

It is a delight to give when the recipient receives it as an act of love rather than something that they think they deserve. God is a giver who seeks "little children" who have the humility to truly be takers.

We need to know that we're truly beautiful. Many of us have relationships that convey this to us. However, if we're honest with ourselves, we know that there are many parts of ourselves that aren't beautiful, parts that we're even ashamed of. However much we try to bury these parts or to convince ourselves that these parts are really OK, on a deeper level we know better.

Therefore, to know that God loves us and always will despite our ugliness and that He's even drawn to us in our brokenness is the assurance we need when the mirror tells us otherwise. This understanding can free us from self-contempt and self-absorption. It can make us jump up and down and cry out with joy to find that we're no longer the ugly duckling. In the next chapter, we'll continue with how brokenness and depression is used by the Master Craftsman.

EXERCISE:

1. How has your perspective affected the way you feel about yourself? About God?

2. What type of perspective are we called to have? Why?

3. Has your brokenness and depression led you to believe that

something was desperately wrong with your relationship with God? How?

4. Is it important to understand the usefulness of our problems in Gods hand? Why?

---

[1] Many will balk at this. My brother who patiently and graciously reviewed this manuscript wrote, "There are people who refer to themselves as 'secular' who take respect for humanity as a primary value." I certainly agree! However, they can't do this in a way *consistent* with their underlying anti-transcendentalism. They are left exclusively with temporal materialism. Denying a transcendental reality, they are left with only one set of eyes, eyes that can only affirm this-world experience. Value is then reduced to the quality of ones friendships, contributions, and the value assigned to the individual by society.

[2] Genesis 1:26-27

[3] Romans 3:10-16

[4] John 3:19

[5] Romans 8:33-34

[6] Romans 8:32

[7] Jeremiah 8:18

[8] Psalm 13:1-2

[9] Psalm 38:7-18

[10] Matthew 26:37-38

[11] Luke 22:44

[12] Instead of "normal," which isn't a Biblical concept, it's essential to understand surrounded by God's love and providential care.

[13] Acts 9:15-16

[14] Matthew 6:24

[15] 2 Corinthians 1:8-9

[16] Romans 5:3-5

[17] The Journey, Os Guinness, Navpress, Colorado Springs, Col., 2001, pg. 38. The quotation comes from Man's Search for Meaning.

[18] The Observing Self, Arthur Deikman, Beacon Press, Boston, 1982.

[19] Isaiah 57:15

[20] Isaiah 66:2

[21] Matthew 5:3
[22] 1 Corinthians 10:12
[23] Romans 5:8-10
[24] Luke 16:14-15
[25] Matthew 23:37
[26] Matthew 18:2-4

CHAPTER 3

How Suffering Renews and Transforms

> "Therefore we do not lose heart. Even though our outward man is perishing, yet the inward man is being renewed day by day. For our light affliction, which is but for a moment, is working for us a far more exceeding and eternal weight of glory, while we do not look at the things which are seen, but at the things which are not seen. For the things which are seen are temporary, but the things which are not seen are eternal." **2 Cor. 4:16-18**

Depression is an auto-immune response. It's not the red blood cells that have become the assailants but our own feelings and thoughts that angrily accuse and attack. Consequently, depression has a hard time seeing beyond the kitchen window to the flowers in the yard. How do we see the flowers?—by *knowing* that, in God's hand, the internal struggle is growing pains and not death blows.

The debacle of 9/11 brought millions of tons of building down. Much of the debris filled the sub-floors of the Twin Towers. It took months to remove the debris. Concrete couldn't just be poured over everything and new buildings erected on top of it. This wouldn't have provided an adequate foundation for the new structures. The only way was to remove the old and to start afresh.

So too with the Christian life! God will not establish us upon the ruins of the old life. The old underlying belief system would inevitably infiltrate, corrupt and leaven the new. Yes, we're purchased and saved upon the old ruins, but before rebuilding can take place in earnest, God will excavate and remove the old. Ordinarily, dynamite, cranes, and blowtorches are the tools of choice to dislodge the old. Trials and suffering are God's tools. The "outward man" must perish as the new arises, but how does this happen? Paul suggests that "affliction" causes us to despair of our hope in the "things which are seen" and reorients us to the "unseen."

The truths of the Gospel can't have their intended, transforming effect while competing ideas and attitudes are alive and well. I believed that I was saved by grace apart from any good deeds, but yet I believed that I was saved because I was more *spiritual* than many others. I knew a good deal when I saw one!

This belief had many offspring. For one thing, I looked down on others because of it. They didn't come to faith because they were more carnally oriented than I. For another, I used it to build myself up in the knowledge of my superior spirituality when I was despairing rather than to resort to the Gospel of God's superiority, which would have told me that I was infinitely beloved for whom I am. Instead, I resorted to the belief in my own superiority. This tended to destroy fellowship instead of creating the unity that God desired. It was also a belief that placed the focus and the hope upon me rather than upon God.

It had to be removed, but how? I clung to the belief of my worthiness and superiority because it was gratifying. The grip of this delusion had to be broken. Could I be lured into loosening my grip by seeing the surpassing beauty of the Gospel? As long as I held on to this belief, I couldn't see the Gospel as it really is. As long as I looked so good to myself, the Gospel didn't seem to offer much that I didn't already have. I had to see the truth about myself, but I was unwilling. My eyes had to be forced to see, and only despairing of self through suffering would accomplish this.

The uniform message of Scripture is that transformation takes place as our thoughts and attitudes change[1] and as we look at the truth of God in Christ.[2] However, we're not receptive to this revelation apart from suffering. Suffering awakens us and causes us to despair of the old beliefs that no longer support us as they had. As failure and despair flexed their intimidating muscles, my prior way of comforting myself through the delusion of my superiority lost its potency. How could I continue in such an absurd belief in face of the onslaughts of devastating panic attacks? Even if I could continue in such a delusion, it couldn't comfort someone who thought he was losing his mind. I needed a major rescue, something my mental gymnastics couldn't provide. I'd have to look towards the Eternal with a depth that I had not previously experienced.

Suffering makes us cry out, "What's wrong; what am I missing?" With new eyes, I began see that my thought-life didn't concur with a true faith in God. One of them had to go and it couldn't be God, not at this point. As light intruded into my darkness, I became ashamed of what I had relied upon. How could I ever have believed with such arrogance and self-conceit? David came to understand that suffering was his teacher. It caused him to look to the eternal light of Scripture.[3]

Paul maintained in his letter to the Corinthian church that suffering and looking towards God should go together. Earlier, he had stated that it was only through suffering that he had come to self-despair and to trust in God.[4] This had to precede any meaningful service. He could only build up others with the very truths he had learned from God through his own suffering.

> "Blessed be the God and Father of our Lord Jesus Christ, the Father of mercies and God of all comfort, who comforts us in all our tribulation, that we may be able to comfort those who are in any trouble, with the comfort with which we ourselves are comforted by God."[5]

We often comfort others in counter-productive ways. When they're confronted with life crushing trials, we tend to resort to either of two tactics. Either we try to reassure them that their trial isn't that threatening, that we've known several people who have successfully gone through this particular trial themselves, or we try to reassure them that *they* are capable of facing the trial.

Although there's nothing wrong with giving them accurate feedback or correcting their mistaken notions, the comfort that we give tends to encourage them toward *self*-trust. Instead of pointing to the Eternal, we help them reinforce their old foundation, the very thing that God is in the process of excavating. In contrast, we need to encourage trust in God. He alone is trustworthy.[6] However, we are unable to do this until God Himself teaches us to trust in Him.

According to Paul, God is preparing us to receive more of His truth and glory. However, there is a qualification. We have to always be ready to distinguish the glory of His presence and truth from our own.[7] We can't take credit for what He gives us. Our very health depends upon it. If God fails to chasten us with self-despair, we'll very gladly deposit His blessings in our private bank account, convinced that we've earned these because of our superiority. To prevent this from happening, God gives us His treasure in "earthen vessels" so it would be clear to everyone that it's about God's superiority and not our own.

Moses had warned the children of Israel that God had given them the strength to acquire wealth.[8] However, there was a grave danger that Israel would take credit for her successes instead of acknowledging God. Indeed, a self-satisfied Israel rejected her God, and her God turned His back upon Israel to Israel's destruction.

We so want to be like God. Perhaps we sense that this is our destiny. John reassured the brethren, "It has not yet been revealed what we shall be, but we know that when He is revealed, *we shall be like Him*, for we shall see Him as He is."[9] We want His glory, and for some reason, God will make sure that we get it, but not right now. He'll do it gradually using suffering as His tool. Paul informed the Corinthians that only through experiencing the sufferings of Christ could they hope to become like Him.[10] We have to be emptied that we might be filled. For now, we must wait. However, we have a tendency of jumping the gun.

How do we endure this time of excavation? —By looking away from the temporal and to the eternal! Suffering takes us in its vice grip and coaxes our gaze away from the temporal, away from our painful circumstances and ourselves. At my first seminary, I was a bit of a star and had no problem focusing contentedly upon myself. However, after I earned my M.A. I went to my second seminary where I had hoped to earn a PhD. Everything went wrong. On the first day, the president spoke to us about his concept of the ideal student. I left devastated. I was the antithesis! According to him, I was the very one who "need not apply."

Many other things happened along the way to undermine my confidence. I found myself struggling through my class work. Despairing of self, I took long walks at night while I cried my eyes out. The God I had believed in up until that time was a small and inadequate god, but my despair of the temporal caused me to cry out in hope of finding a greater God, One who could make up for all of my deficiencies. Believing against evidence to the contrary, I found that such a God was listening all along.

We will all encounter times when the only evidence is that which is provided by Scripture. Sight takes us no further than our mangled lives, and understanding has skipped town. At these times, only a Scripture-fed faith can penetrate the gloom and ascend to the Eternal; only Scripture can reassure us that we're on course.

EXERCISE:

1. Have you discarded any beliefs after you've seen that they are inconsistent with Scripture? Which beliefs? Did suffering play an important role?

2. Do you presently have any beliefs that are inconsistent with Scripture? What are you doing about them?

3. What has helped you to trust in God?

---

[1] Romans 12:2
[2] 2 Corinthians 4:4, 6; 2 Cor. 3:18
[3] Psalm 119:67
[4] 2 Corinthians 1:8-10
[5] 2 Corinthians 1:3-4
[6] John 15:4-5
[7] 2 Corinthians 4:7
[8] Deuteronomy 8:18
[9] 1 John 3:2
[10] 2 Corinthians 4:10-11

CHAPTER 4

Dangers of Self-Righteousness

> "Behold I, Paul, say to you that if you receive circumcision, Christ will be of no benefit to you. And I testify again to every man who receives circumcision, that he is under obligation to keep the whole Law. You have been severed from Christ, you who are seeking to be justified by law; you have fallen from grace." **Galatians 5:2-4**

Depression is hope-starved. The source of its hope, the self, is being brutally murdered. Its boundaries are continually overrun by unstoppable marauders. Our own feelings have become assailants, our thoughts disdainful prosecutors looking for the final conviction. We need a new hope, a hope in a Power greater than ourselves. Self-righteousness is the lingering regime of the old hope. It's antithetical to the new, and we need to *understand* this! It says, "I can do it; I deserve it!" It tells God, "I don't need You; I can build my own Tower of Babel to reach the heavens. I don't want You. You get in the way of the thoughts I want to think and the things I want to do." It rejects the new hope, and God reciprocates.[1] Therefore, in order to fully bask in the new, the old has to be swept away.

When at Berkeley at the tender and not too gracious age of 20, my girlfriend and I were invited by her friend at attend a recital of Schumann's A minor piano concerto. Stuart, her boy friend, was the pianist. Afterwards, we all went out for a coffee.

It wasn't long before Stuart (pseudonym) asked us what we thought of the Schumann piece. I jumped at the opportunity. "I think it could have been performed with more enunciation."

Stuart was pained by my response, but I had succeeded in my mission. I had made it clear that I knew Schumann well enough to make some comparative judgments. I was a music savant! Whether my judgments were correct or not wasn't the issue. My problem was that I was determined to establish my self-righteous *value* as a person by promoting myself as a music critic, and it didn't matter who I stepped on.

By attempting to build my own Tower of Babel, I was turning my back upon any hope of God's righteousness. The two pursuits are mutually exclusive. Paul warns the Galatian church that if they are trusting in themselves, they are not trusting in God and are alienated from Him. They couldn't do both! They had trusted in Christ and had received the free gift of salvation apart from anything they had done to merit it. But they had been introduced to a new theology. Trust in Christ was great, but as any reasonable person understood, they must also perform the good deeds of the Law in order to make their salvation a reality. They had to trust in both Christ's righteousness and their own. In their particular case, they had to become Jews through circumcision and follow the Mosaic Law. It was now up to *them*. God had done His part.

Sadly, they were very eager to exchange a simple trust in God for a trust in their own performance with a sprinkling of God's righteousness on the side. In their unsuspecting zeal, they were like fresh soldiers itching for the challenge of front-line combat, unable to visualize the costs imposed by warfare. Likewise, as I took upon myself the mantle of a music critic, I couldn't see how this elevated status would cost me dearly further down the road.

What are the costs? By rejecting the gift of God's righteousness in favor of our own, we are telling God several things He doesn't want to hear: "My righteous performance, although far from perfect, is an adequate payment for salvation. God now owes me. I'm therefore 'deserving' of God and superior to all the others who fail to make the grade. Also, this notion of a 'gift' isn't at all just. I prefer the idea that I'm being saved because I deserve it, and others are lost because they too deserve what they're getting."

This is the posture of arrogance and the unwillingness to face the truth about our true status. It's unwilling to see self and God and therefore contorts His true image to suit itself. To maintain this posture, we have to harden our hearts against the voice within. It told me, "you're not a music critic. You know little about music. You just want the accolades without the necessary work. You want to look good in the eyes of others. This is your god! It's about 'you' and nobody else!" How could I listen to such a voice of truth? It was devastating! I had to harden my heart against it!

When we harden our heart against truth, we harden it against God. Self-deception is the way of humanity, its very best specimens. The Pharisees were Israel's leading candidates. They had the respect of the people. If they weren't saved, it was clear that no one could be. However Jesus saw something else deep within their hearts.

> "When therefore you give alms, do not sound a trumpet before you, as the hypocrites do in the synagogues and in the streets, that they may be honored by men. Truly I say to you, they have their reward in full."[2]

Why did the Pharisees pursue honor from others? Self-righteousness can never be secure in itself. It is insatiable. Somewhat aware of its own illusory existence, it must continually to justify itself, and therefore requires a steady diet of affirmations. Proverbs tells us that this tendency is ubiquitous.

> "Every man's way is right in his own eyes,
> But the Lord weighs the hearts."[3]

The more we get, the more we want. Hitting a home run with bases loaded might give us a temporary high, but that's all it is. It never delivers the pay-off that it promises. We can never receive enough compliments or promotions. Our bank account can never be big enough nor our performance stellar enough. Thus, pursuit for the ultimate fix!

In this pursuit, we become increasingly alienated from ourselves, the truth, and from God, and we seem to do this so eagerly. In receiving their "full reward" in the form of the respect of man, the Pharisees had forfeited a relationship with the source of all hope and joy.

Depression puts a loaded gun to our head and desperately demands a rescue. Sadly, this rescue often entails the reconstruction of the old self-esteem edifice with its insatiable appetite. It is the identical rut of self-absorption that has led to failure so many times previously. Instead, depression requires a release from the tyranny of self.

This moribund edifice not only alienates us from self and God, but it also alienates us from others. As an eight grader, I had taken a test that I was very concerned about. I was ecstatic to find that I had received an "A." However, my ecstasy was short lived. I later discovered that most of the others had received "A+." I was crushed. It's hard to enjoy others when you're constantly comparing yourself to them.

The Schumann piano concerto had made a music critic out of me, and that felt good. However, I was destined to meet some truly erudite music critics. Rather than appreciating their contribution to my limited understanding, I resented them. Next to them, my comparative worth was diminished. The taller we make ourselves, the harder the fall! Had I never inflated myself to believe that I was a savant, I wouldn't have felt threatened by a true savant, or even by an aspiring one.

Self-righteousness produces an avalanche of psychological pains, and it should! It should hurt when we place our hand down upon a hot stove. Pain protects. Leprosy merely deprives it's victims of pain, but pain is a master teacher. It tells us when we're using our limbs the wrong way or when we're scratching an itch too hard or picking too strenuously at a sore. Without pain, our extremities go unprotected and eventually decay.

Pain also provides relational protection. A guilty conscience may warn us when we've treated another badly and when we need to apologize. A guilty conscience may salvage a relationship. Psychological pain is also critical to our most significant relationship. It might warn us when our attitudes towards God are incorrect and relationship-denying. Endorsing our own righteousness is a rejection of God's righteousness. It is tantamount to turning our life over to a light-sucking monster who leaves us in the darkness of our own arrogance.

Depression is a cultivated field. Its destitution provides promise of new growth. This is because we have a Savior who delights in impossible rescues. Following the crucifixion, when His disciples had disowned the faith and were running in fear, this Savior made them do an "about face" with His resurrection. From the deepest gloom, from the lowest pit of despair and failure, He raised them to new heights. He says the same to all the broken: "Come to Me, all who are weary and heavy-laden, and I will give you rest."[4]

BUT DOESN'T THE BIBLE TALK A LOT ABOUT THE NECESSITY FOR OBEDIENCE?

Truly, we are called upon to live like Jesus lived, but we endeavor to live faithfully not to *earn* salvation, but because we have salvation. Obedience isn't the cause of salvation or of God's love but the *result*. It's not the root but the fruit of salvation. Our faithfulness follows God's faithfulness, it doesn't precede it. John asserts that we love God because he first loved us.[5] Radical discipleship isn't optional, but its motivation must be consistent with the truth about our broken selves. The motivation of love and gratitude best manifest this truth.

We really have to banish any idea that we can earn anything from God. For one thing, no one has ever succeeded at this.[6] It wouldn't therefore be rational to place any hope in such an enterprise. For another thing, God is never in a position that He owes anyone anything. The expectation that we can present Him with a bill for services rendered and demand payment is unthinkable. Paul confirms that one aspect of the greatness of God is that no one can give Him something that He needs. He'll never be beholden to anyone.[7] Everything we receive from God is based upon His grace, not our merit.

James tells us quite explicitly that, if we play the performance game, *one* misstep will condemn us as if we were guilty in all regards.[8] To the contrary, God deserves all thanksgiving because everything good comes from Him rather than by virtue of any merit of our own.[9] If there was anything that we did earn, it would follow logically that God doesn't deserve all the praise. We too would deserve some. Instead, Jesus taught that even if we had done everything we were commanded to do, we should consider ourselves "unworthy servants."[10]

BUT DON'T WE REAP WHAT WE SOW?

Often, the Bible does affirm the following relationship:

$$\text{SOWING} \longrightarrow \text{REAPING}$$

It would seem that this formula should deny God from getting all the credit. It seems that we should get at least some of it! However, this relationship doesn't give us the complete picture. Paul explained that whatever he became was purely a function of the grace of God. Although he worked harder than all the other Apostles, he couldn't take any credit for it because he recognized that even his sowing, his efforts, had been granted him by God.[11] Hence, the following relationship emerges:

GRACE ⟶ SOWING ⟶ REAPING

The more we grow into the truth that we are completely in His Hand, that we are His workmanship, and that He truly guides us into paths of righteousness, the more of the peace of God we will experience. This understanding takes the weight off of our backs and places all of our hopeful attention upon God.

For so many years, although I did have the grace of God in my life, I felt that I had a critical fault that always deprived me of the blessings that God wanted to give me. As hard as I would try to overcome this fault, the more frustrated and despairing I became, convinced that this fault negated the grace of God. This is because I didn't have an adequate understanding of God.

Many of us welcome into our unsuspecting bosom an anxiety-producing, self-focused theology. Instead, when we see God as He truly is, it produces real gratitude and adoration, a worship that lifts us out of ourselves and connects us intimately and joyously to God. We understand that there is no sin, weakness, or infirmity that God finds insurmountable. This is the faith that overcomes, one that worships Him as He is, in "Spirit and in truth."[12]

Convincing people that self-righteousness blinds, kills, and alienates from God is a "hard sell." The last thing we are willing to see about ourselves is that we are utterly unworthy of anything from God and deserve only condemnation. This flies in the face of everything we've ever told ourselves. God has to make it real for us, and it's going to be a painful process. It was for Nebuchadnezzar, the great empire-builder of Babylon, in the 6th century BC. Babylon was the greatest power of its day and its king was resting comfortably upon his successes and impregnability until he had a disturbing dream. He called for his wise men, who were unable to interpret it. Then Daniel arrived on the scene. Reluctantly, he rendered the interpretation. Nebuchadnezzar would be struck down with insanity for seven years, thinking himself to be a cow, until he came to realize that everything he had came from God and not from himself as he always supposed.

The following year, we find the king upon the roof of his

palace overlooking magnificent Babylon, congratulating himself for all his great accomplishments, when he heard a voice: "King Nebuchadnezzar, to you it is spoken: the kingdom has departed from you! And they shall drive you from men, and your dwelling shall be with the beasts of the field. They shall make you eat grass like oxen; and seven times (years) shall pass over you, until you know that the Most High rules in the kingdom of men, and gives it to Whomever He chooses."[13]

After the seven years, the king was restored to both his sanity and to his kingdom and proclaimed for the world to hear, "All the inhabitants of the earth are reputed as nothing. He does according to His will…No one can restrain His hand or say to Him, 'What have you done.'"[14]

All this happened to Nebuchadnezzar in order that he would learn a truth about himself and about God. Yes, it would make him act more morally seeing that he didn't possess the "divine right of kings" to do whatever they wanted to do. He now knew that he had an all-powerful Godfather who had set him up, to whom he owed every allegiance.

This knowledge of God's loving power is precious and surpasses in value everything else.[15] It's also *necessary* if we're going to live with crushing defeats. It tells the depressed soul, "You can rest in Me. Yes, your situation might be hopeless from a human perspective, but I am the source of all hope." It may be humbling to find, as the king had found, that it wasn't about him but about the One who chose him. However, it's this knowledge that allows us to take our obsessive eyes off ourselves and our hopeless circumstances. In this knowledge we find an anchor for our fears.

We don't come to this knowledge on our own. Don't worry about having to manufacture a certain state of mind. It is granted to the seeker. Paul reassured the Philippian church that if they were predisposed to think in erroneous ways, God would correct them.[16] Ridding ourselves of the ubiquitous tentacles of self-righteousness is a continual process, which was jeopardized by the presence of the Circumcision party. As was the case in Galatia, the Philippians were falsely instructed that faith wasn't enough. They also had to become Jews through circumcision and then to perform the Law for their keep. In contrast to this, Paul assured the church that the believer in Christ should not put any *trust* in their performance.[17]

Using himself as an example, he first sets forth his pedigree and accomplishments arguing that if anyone had reason to trust in themselves and their righteous attainments before God, Paul had more. But rather than resting upon these laurels, he took the view that they were *counterproductive*; not that education and good deeds are bad (they certainly aren't!), but that *trusting* in them precludes trusting in Christ. He therefore counted them as garbage as a means of merit before God. Paul stated that this understanding was necessary in order to "be found in Him, not having my own righteousness, which is from the law (performance righteousness), but that which is through faith in Christ, the righteousness which is from God by faith."[18]

How do we deal with the self-righteousness we find within ourselves? We can't force it out, but, according to Paul, we can begin to regard it for what it is. We can expose the deceptions of this alternate righteousness we've constructed for ourselves, recognizing how it has enslaved us to a false hope and, even now keeps us away from a fuller enjoyment of our riches in Christ.

It's a process. Paul admits he hasn't arrived. We get the sense that as he sees the vestiges of self-righteousness in his own life, he *continues* to regard them as "dung" so that he might have a deeper intimacy with Christ.[19]

The fundamental work is in the mind, what we believe. Only afterwards, are we exhorted to live a life consistent with the insights we've been granted.[20] Once we are assured that our own righteousness, honor, worth, and significance are a "done deal" in Christ, we can begin to devote ourselves to the needs for worth and respect of others.

Granted, it may not feel this way and it may be a struggle to maintain this perspective. Old habits die slowly, and the opposition from our other nature is palpable. However, the more we look away from temporal considerations to our heavenly Treasure, the more our heart will follow. Allow Scripture to continue to inform your beliefs about what matters and what, in comparison, doesn't matter.

1. It doesn't matter how deserving we are. God chooses the losers.[21]

2. It doesn't matter how sinful we've been. No one can top Paul. He not only killed Christians, but forced them to renounce their faith. God saving Paul exemplifies the truth the God's love can reach down to the most putrid sewer.[22]

3. It doesn't matter how poor our performance. God's love isn't going away.[23]

EXERCISE: To stay afloat in a storm, a sailboat might be forced to jettison some of its non-essential baggage.

1. What baggage of self-righteousness have you thrown overboard?
2. How did this affect you?
3. Are there yet ways that you are esteeming yourself more highly than you ought (Rom. 12:3)?
4. How has an inflated estimation of yourself caused you hurt?
5. How can you help others release some of their unnecessary baggage?

---

[1] Romans 1:28
[2] Matthew 6:2
[3] Proverbs 21:2
[4] Matthew 11:28
[5] 1 John 4:19
[6] Romans 3:19-20
[7] Romans 11:35

[8] James 2:10

[9] James 1:17

[10] Luke 17:10

[11] 1 Corinthians 15:9-10

[12] John 4:24

[13] Daniel 4:31-32

[14] Daniel 4:35-36

[15] Jeremiah 9:23-24

[16] Philippians 3:15

[17] Philippians 3:3

[18] Philippians 3:9

[19] Philippians 3:8

[20] Philippians 3:16

[21] 1 Corinthians 1:26-30

[22] 1 Timothy 1:15-16

[23] Romans 8:38-39

CHAPTER 5

Negative Transformation

> "We all with unveiled face, beholding as in a mirror the glory of God are being transformed into the same image from glory to glory, just as by the Spirit of the Lord" **(2 Cor. 3:18)**

Recently a student asked me a question that is reverberating from one church to the next: "Why are there so many unhappy Christians?" My response was an easy one. "Many Christians simply don't understand God as they aught."

I had tried on for size many different beliefs about God, many destructive to my own psychological well-being." In my mind, God was like the Marines. He was looking for just a few good men, and I wasn't one of them. It's no surprise that I felt rejected by such a God.

If we believe in a God who is out to get us, it's clearly going to affect the way we feel about God and also how our lives take shape. In a recent study, 600 participants were compared. One group thought that God was either punishing or abandoning them. Within the next two years, this group experienced a 30% higher mortality rate than the control group.[1]

What we believe about God matters. We long to be transformed, to leave behind the temptations, reactions, and depression. Jesus also assured His disciples that as they continued to follow Him, they'd know the truth, which would transform them.[2] This "knowledge" isn't a one time thing. We're not at liberty to merely know it and then to forget about it. As the above verses state, this is knowledge to behold and embrace.

However, there are many other things that we behold, things upon which we place our hopes. What we trust determines who we are and who we'll become. Insofar as we are being transformed into the image of God as we trust in Him, we are also being transformed into the image of whatever it is that we trust. A.W. Tozer wrote, "The history of mankind will probably show that no people have ever risen above its religion, and man's history will positively demonstrate that no religion has ever been greater than its idea of God...We tend by a secret law of the soul to move toward our mental image of God."[3]

Tozer's assertion is borne out in many ways. We find that belief in an arbitrary God produces followers who are undependable; belief in a harsh God produces insensitive followers. We also see in the case of children how the apple doesn't fall far from the tree. We also find that role models, whether they're respectable or not, exert powerful influences upon their admirers. We become like whatever it is that we admire.

The process takes time. A professional from a largely Muslim African nation told me about the many beautiful Christians he had met. Then he warned me that he had also met many wonderful Muslims in his own country. I couldn't dispute this fact, but this shouldn't be taken at face value either. Clearly, the more serious one is about Christ, the more that person becomes like Christ; likewise, the more serious one is about Mohammed, the more he too will become like Mohammed.

However, the contrast between their lives is striking. In one Hadith (an authoritative saying of Mohammed), a "Jew and a Jewess who had committed fornication" were brought before Mohammed who instructed them to bring him their Torah. They then had to read the passage against fornication. The Jewish man covered the section which prescribes stoning and read around it. His ruse discovered, he was told to lift his hand, revealing the verse about stoning. "The Messenger of God gave the order, and they were stoned."[4]

What we admire makes or breaks us. Hosea writes, "The Lord said, 'When I found you, it was like finding fresh grapes in the desert! When I saw your ancestors, it was like seeing the first ripe grapes of the season! But then they deserted Me for Baal-Peor, giving themselves to that shameful idol. Soon they *became* as vile as the god they worshiped."[5] Israel rebelled against God in favor of Baal-Peor. Looking to this god, they *became* like him. Where we place our heart and our hopes has profound consequences upon our development.

Paul gives us another portrait of this phenomenon.

"For the wrath of God is revealed from heaven against all ungodliness and unrighteousness of men, who suppress the truth in unrighteousness, because what may be known of God is manifest in them, for God has shown it to them. For since the creation of the world His invisible attributes are clearly seen, being understood by the things that are made, even His eternal power and Godhead, so that they are without excuse, because, although they knew God, they did not glorify Him as God...and changed the glory of the incorruptible God into an image made like corruptible man—and birds and four-footed animals and creeping things. Therefore *God also gave them up* (emphasis mine) to uncleanness, in the lusts of their hearts, to dishonor their bodies among themselves,...For this reason *God gave them up to vile passions*...they did not like to retain God in their knowledge, *God gave them over to a debased mind*, to do those things which are not fitting."[6]

Humanity rejects "beholding" God; God "gives them up" to those things they so desire to worship, and they inherit the consequences of their worship. Fittingly, they become degraded by the thing they adore.

Whenever we reject the light, we reject our true nourishment and seek a substitute that inevitably leads to degradation. The effects are relational, psychological, and physical. The dying process begins as we pull away from God and He from us. Cut off from the only source of life and nourishment, we begin to decay. As our object of worship changes, so too our thoughts and passions. As positive transformation is a process, so too is the gloomy portrait Paul paints in Romans 1.

WHAT ARE THE MECHANICS OF THIS DYING PROCESS?

I think, at this point, we need to introduce that vilified 'S' word, Sin. Sin is not merely an act. In fact, the worst part of sin isn't the outward manifestation, but everything that proceeds and follows it. There's an entire process involved. When we sin and fail to repent, we become entangled in webs of self-justifications and rationalizations. We endeavor to convince ourselves that our rationalizations are correct and that our conscience is wrong. Our conscience however preaches such a persuasive message that we have to shut it down or at least suppress its light. This distances us from God and relegates us into darkness.

Let me go out on a limb of the tree of the knowledge of good and evil in hopes of demonstrating that the sin that kills is far more than an action, it's a process that seduces, deceives, and kills. Our first parents knew not to eat from this tree. They knew from their very Creator and Sustainer that they'd die. Yet the Serpent deceived Eve into believing that God had been holding out on them because He wanted everything for Himself. She embraced the tempting lie and her behavior accordingly fell into line. We live according to the way we think and believe. Then Adam followed suit, although he knew better.[7]

Amidst such virgin territory, the effects of sin came down upon them like a sledgehammer: "Then the eyes of both of them were opened, and they knew that they were naked; and they sewed fig leaves together and made themselves coverings."[8] They were so overwhelmed by a sense of shame and guilt; their response was history's first cover up. They responded by trying to cover over their guilt.

Their response seems laughable to us: making clothes from leaves! Couldn't they see that such a measure could only be temporary at best? Didn't they know that their ploy would be uncovered? (Our own self-righteous maneuvers are little different. We think that we've covered ourselves pretty darn well. Meanwhile, everyone else can see how full of ourselves we are.) Wouldn't it have just been a lot easier to say, "God, I screwed up; have mercy on me?"

To make matters worse, they hid from God when they heard Him. It was foolhardy enough to try to hide the sin, but now the cover-up expanded to the point of trying to hide themselves! Sin is an aggressive cancer. If it's not removed, it continues to grow. It never reaches a point where it is satisfied. Some invading viruses are so successful because they are able to disguise themselves as host cells to avoid the immune system. Sin is even worse. It is able to capture our minds and degrade both their ability to reason and to detect a foreign threat. How else can we explain our First Couple's unreasonableness in thinking they could cover their sin and then hide from the Omnipotent Creator? How else can we explain their unwillingness to confess their sin and to cast themselves upon the mercies of God, especially because they were facing imminent death? The unbeliever is equally unreasonable. Confronted with the prospect of an eternity, reason would demand that they at least ask the important questions![9]

Their sin had overwhelmed them with guilt and shame. Isn't it reasonable that they'd want to vomit up and out the cause of this shame and forever flee from such filth? (Looking back upon our lives, there are many things we had embraced that we now feel ashamed of.)

Instead, they advanced up the ladder of death; the cover-up advanced to lies and self-justification. God called out to Adam, "Where are you?" God knew where they were, but His question offered Adam an opportunity to confess. Instead of admitting the sin and the cover-up, Adam obfuscated, "I was afraid because I was naked and hid myself."[10] Perhaps his half-truth would satisfy God and maybe elicit a little pity? God pursued the real issue, "Have you eaten from the tree...?"[11] Surely, Adam would now take responsibility seeing that he was caught with his hand in the cookie jar! Only a fool would continue to play games with God.

Adam had the perfect excuse: "The woman whom *You gave to me* (emphasis mine), she gave me of the tree and I did eat."[12] Self-justification places the cause of the sin elsewhere, this time in God's lap. God was at fault! What ungratefulness, blaming God for His grace in providing Adam with a companion!

Eve failed to learn from Adam's pathetic blame shifting, instead of seizing the opportunity to confess the mess. By this time, she was equally basking in sin's deception and death. She too justified herself by blaming the Serpent.

Clearly, the Light had become a great discomfort. The Presence of God, which had been a great source of light and of love, had now become Someone to avoid. They chose "escape from the Presence of God" instead of confession and repentance and God granted them their hearts' desire and mercifully banished them from His Presence. Had they repented, human history might have been very different, but such is the power and dominion of sin.

Once we embrace sin, we can no longer face the Light to avail ourselves of His healing and transformation. Either, we are trusting in God or else in our own self-justifying manipulations—a flight from the light. It's one or the other. Fleeing from His very Presence is antithetical to basking in His light. We can't adore God as we're fleeing from Him. These two activities are mutually exclusive. You can choose only one.

It's possible that Paul had Adam and Eve in mind when he wrote, "And even as they did not like to retain God in their knowledge, God gave them over to a debased mind, to do those things which are not fitting."[13] When we cease to behold God, we begin to decay. In our self-imposed dying, God doesn't have to punish us. We reap the fruits of the death we've chosen for ourselves. When we flee from God's light and truth, we're going to bang our heads in the darkness.

"Because they hated knowledge…They would have none of My counsel and despised My every rebuke. Therefore, they shall eat the fruit of their own way, and will be filled to the full with their own fancies."[14]

The confused couple consistently failed to confess their transgression. As a result, they burrowed all the more deeply into the darkness of their own devices. Ironically, they derived what they wanted—escape from the Light into the briars of their own self-appointed exile.

Modern man is afflicted with confusion and seeks to run from it through distractions and an unwillingness to think deeply. The Genesis of our hollow existence is reflected back to us through the experiences of Adam and Eve. By rejecting God and His Word and by failing to repent, they also rejected their source of being, love, and worth. The result was guilt and anxiety. They tried to deal with this problem in their own way. They resorted to hiding and to their own devices to handle the guilt/anxiety problem, their own works—fig leaves. Having embarked on a divergent course from God, they then had to resort to justifications. Loosing their worth or righteousness, they needed to come up with a new source of worth with whatever web of rationalizations and justifications that are necessary to make this new unnatural source credible.

Each time that we sin and fail to confess and repent, we too have to produce a fig-leaf substitute for our lost innocence. The gaping cavity cries out to be covered by a combination of good works and rationalizations. Inevitably, it constitutes a flight from the Light into darkness and death. The price of feeling comfortable is purchased through the destruction of the conscience. The Light buried, negative transformation reigns. We "look" for God and find only ourselves.

We adopt a new identity based upon performance, popularity, beauty, or from whatever else we might derive worth or significance. However, these never suffice as well as the original Source of worth. Some aren't able to meet their own performance standards. Only a certain percentage will be recognized as beautiful or popular. We may have to resort to delusion or even to hallucination to give us that sense of worth we so desperately crave. John

Modrow argues that schizophrenic hallucination is self-generated to compensate for a loss of self-esteem and its accompanying panic.[15] If he's correct, this so profoundly exhibits our need for significance, why we reject reality in favor of a comfortable fantasy. It also explains why we'll resort to murder more quickly when our honor has been assailed than when our car has been stolen.

Furthermore, this sense of significance that we derive from our performance is short lived. We always need a greater fix to give us that previous sense of significance. Increasingly, we require others to affirm us and become defensive when they don't. We place intolerable demands upon ourselves and upon our relationships to give us our worth.

Ignorant of sin and its dynamics, secular clinical practice often tries to improve our fig leaves rather than removing them to get at the core of the problem. Instead of helping the sufferer come to the truth about his situation, secularism is often content to bless the rationalizations through building the client's self-esteem. This merely serves to enable the client to be more comfortable with their darkness.

WHAT MUST WE DO TO FREE OURSELVES FROM THE GRIP OF SIN?

1. Recognize the power, destructiveness, and devices of sin and how we are degraded by it.

2. Seek the counsel of others who can be more objective about our situation. "The ear that hears the rebukes of life will abide among the wise. He who disdains instruction despises his own soul, but he who heeds rebuke gets understanding. The fear of the Lord is the instruction of wisdom, and before honor goes humility" (Proverbs 15:31-33). God will raise us up and comfort us after we acknowledge the painful truth about ourselves.

3. Confront the truth about ourselves. "Behold, You desire truth

in the inward parts, and in the hidden part You will make me to know wisdom" (Psalm 51:6). David is said to have penned this Psalm following his sin with Bathsheba. The truth he was talking about was the truth of his own sins and cover-up. This was the precondition for the reestablishment of his relationship with his God.

4. Take full responsibility for sin. James warns, " Let no one say when he is tempted, 'I am tempted by God'; for God can't be tempted by evil, nor does He Himself tempt anyone. But each is tempted when he is drawn away by his own desires and enticed. Then, when desire has conceived, it gives birth to sin; and sin, when it's full-grown, brings forth death" (1:13-15). Blame shifting is unacceptable, even when it was another who started the cycle of sin.

5. Come clean and receive full restoration. John assures us that, no matter how many times we sin, "If we confess our sins, He is faithful and just to forgive us our sin and to cleanse us from all unrighteous" (1 John 1:9). Honesty nurtures our soul better than a thousand creative devices.

All of this sounds very negative to our western ears. Christianity has been termed "dirty-rotten-sinner religion" by its detractors. There is some truth to this charge, but the important question is not whether it's depressing but whether it's true and whether these insights will lead to reconciliation with our Maker and Redeemer.

An old and dear friend, who has been very influenced by the wisdom of secular psychology, wrote that she thought that I was all too negative and self-critical and that I was making myself depressed though my negative fixation. I responded to her with the following letter:

"I can understand what you say about not wanting to hate yourself anymore. For you the answer is to focus upon the positive about yourself. As you know, self-contempt has always been a strong tendency in my own life. But I found that trying to elevate myself thrust me back squarely into the quagmire of self-contempt. The more I struggled against self-loathing through building my self-esteem, the more the internal struggle became inflamed. I found that I was still ensnarled in the same focus upon self and self's performance; promoting myself and surrounding myself with others who would promote me, or at least trying to surround myself with such people. My peace was continually shattered by my constant attempts to justify myself. I was addicted to whatever it was that would give me the 'fix' that I needed, and I always needed more of it. The same 'fix' just wouldn't do the trick.

I subsequently found peace in just admitting to myself and to God that I was worthless apart from Him and didn't deserve anything from Him: 'So likewise you, when you have done all those things which you are commanded, say, 'We are unprofitable servants. We have done what was our duty to do.''[16]

In one sense, I gave in to the self-loathing to find that it produced a greater relief and appreciation for God: 'Therefore I say to you, her sins, *which are* many, are forgiven, for she loved much. But to whom little is forgiven, *the same* loves little.'[17] When I forsook trying to lift myself up, I found that God in His Mercy would do it for me.

There is a relief in knowing that it's no longer about me and my own personal righteousness or worthiness: 'But what things were gain to me, these I have counted loss for Christ. Yet indeed I also count all things loss for the excellence of the knowledge of Christ Jesus my Lord, for whom I have suffered the loss of all things, and count them as rubbish, that I may gain Christ and be found in Him, not having my own righteousness, which *is* from the law, but that which *is* through faith in Christ, the righteousness which is from God by faith.'[18]

If I felt worthy, I wouldn't adore Him as I ought.

It is only in my utter brokenness that He is worshiped as He ought to be: 'I have been crucified with Christ; it is no longer I who live, but Christ lives in me; and the *life* which I now live in the flesh I live by faith in the Son of God, who loved me and gave Himself for me.'[19]

It might sound depressing, but I found that humbling actually meant eventual encouragement: 'Therefore humble yourselves under the mighty hand of God, that He may exalt you in due time, casting all your care upon Him, for He cares for you.'[20] As distasteful as this might sound, I'm convinced that this is God's way."

If one party has grievously offended another, it does little good for the offending party to ignore the offense or to even buy the offended one generous gifts. Even if he succeeds in seducing the offended party into receiving the gifts, the offended will generally remain unsatisfied until the offender humbles himself to deal with the problem by confessing his wrongdoing. Repentance must precede reconciliation. Where there is unfinished business, any new business hastily thrust upon the agenda will become tainted by the old. We can't impose our ways upon God. The issue of the truth of our real status must first be dealt with. Although our sins are many, reconciliation with God is just a prayer away.

EXERCISE: Shipwrecks generally don't result from a single miscalculation. There are usually a series of mistakes. Often, sin is a process; the better we can identify it, the better prepared we will be for its next assault.

1. What sinful patterns have you been able to identify in your own lives.

2. What effects has unconfessed sin had upon you? How has it affected your relationship with God?

3. What have been the results of confessing sin that you had

been justifying?

---

[1] Kenneth Pargamet, BGS University

[2] John 8:31

[3] Knowledge of the Holy

[4] James P. Gudel, "Christian Research Journal," Vol. 27, Number 1, pg. 38. Compare this with John 8:1-11.

[5] Hosea 9:10

[6] Rom. 1:18-28

[7] 1 Tim. 2:14

[8] Gen. 3:7

[9] "Pascal's Wager"

[10] Genesis 3:10

[11] Gen. 3:11

[12] Gen. 3:12

[13] Rom. 1:28

[14] Proverbs 1:29-31

[15] How to Become a Schizophrenic

[16] Luke 17:10

[17] Luke 7:47

[18] Phil. 3:7-9

[19] Gal. 2:20

[20] 1 Peter 5:6-7

CHAPTER 6

Christ Ennobles

> "Do you not know that your body is the temple of the Holy Spirit who is in you, whom you have from God, and you are not you own?" 1 Cor. 6:17

In the early eighties, Bob Dylan sung, "You gotta serve somebody." He touched upon an important truth. We're built for service. It's only a question of, "Whom do we serve." Absolute freedom is an illusion. I once tried to play a game of chess without any rules with a friend. The game came abruptly to an unsatisfactory end with pieces scattered all over the place. Without limitations or rules, we couldn't play chess with any degree of satisfaction.

It's not reasonable to expect to find a life without service or other limitations. We maximize our freedom as we learn to accept our limitations. It would be equally unreasonable for a goldfish to leave his bowl in pursuit of freedom. The goldfish maximizes its freedom by staying within the limitations of water. Outside its bowl, it can only flap wildly as it gasps for breath. If we were created to find satisfaction through service, we maximize our freedom by accepting our script and living within its confines.

Like the goldfish, we too seek our freedom outside the fish bowl. We can't escape service any more than we can escape breathing.

Ironically, we seek our sense of worth by serving fickle others or by achieving success through socially approved channels. We come to rely upon objects that can't satisfy. The exalted expectations we place open these relationships or these sources of esteem ensures their demise. We strangle our relationships and resent those upon whom we've become dependent. They, in turn, abhor our dependence. We so crave success and approval that we either drive them far away or become addicted to them.

We were made to serve One who will not disappoint. He exults in our dependence upon Him like a father does when his child trustingly slips her hand into his own when crossing a busy intersection. While co-dependency is a psychological trap, dependency upon our Savior suits us like a carefully cobbled shoe. Jesus referred to Himself as "The Good Shepherd." When the chips are down and the threat is near, others will abandon their flock. Not only will Jesus not abandon His flock, He will actually lay down His own life for His dependent sheep.[1]

It bears mentioning that sheep are thoroughly vulnerable. They lack speed, strength, and any form of defense by which to repel enemies. Furthermore, they can't even take care of themselves. They can't remove the briars from their wool, and they can't recover themselves when they end up on their backs and thrash about helplessly if they're in only a slight depression.

It should be no surprise that we're likened to sheep who need a shepherd. We're plagued with all sorts of psychological afflictions that we can't manage. Often, we are even oblivious to the afflictions.

As His children, we've been lifted to our feet and made into His priests and kings. There are no longer human priests who serve as our intermediaries.[2] We don't have to approach our Redeemer through the good pleasure of a fickle, biased priest who might elect to use his power to abuse. We don't have to worm our way into anybody's good graces or to win anyone's approval, because we have His approval. Those who regard us as vulnerable sheep and wish to prey upon us fall prey to their own venom. Consequently, we reserve all our adoration and devotion for the only One who deserves it. Yes, we're called upon to submit to one another in love, but this is something that we offer freely without any attitude of subservience or inferiority.

Christ directs us to dispense with the terminology of status. He forbids us to call anyone rabbi or teacher because there is only One who should occupy this superior station in our lives.[3]

Yes, I am a teacher and I don't mind that anyone introduces me as his or her teacher, but I do object when they call me "professor" or "teacher." I may have greater expertise in teaching, but this doesn't make me the superior human being as a title tends to suggest.

We shouldn't perform obeisance to another human. The Israelite kings had to keep a copy of the Law and to read it daily "that his heart be not lifted up above that of his brethren."[4] They might have been king, but they were still human beings like everyone else. We are all brethren and share the same ultimate worth regardless of our station in life.[5] We need not grovel before any dignitary. In fact, were we to do this, we would dishonor our one Dignitary. We can serve only One master and are warned against adopting a second one. "You were bought at a price; do not become slaves of men."[6] This should make us circumspect about our employment situations.

The significance that God places upon us is unbelievable. It certainly was to David. He was awestruck by God's concern for us in view of the extensiveness and grandeur of the heavens and stars, "For You have made him but little lower than the angels."[7] Through Hosea the prophet, He declared His undying love for His people in a way that's embarrassing to us by virtue of its intimacy. He will marry His people so that they'll finally know Him.[8] Paul makes a similar revelation when he compares human marriage to a marriage with God suggesting that the Church is connected to Christ in a way analogous to a man's connection to his wife.[9]

I used to feel so intimidated in the presence of accomplished people, that it was almost painful. I no longer have to run away as I once did; I have been made one spirit with my Redeemer.[10] If we are God's, the most important and powerful Being imaginable, we are arrayed with significance and reek with status. Paul claims that we supernaturally exude the fragrance of Christ as we serve as His ambassadors.[11] Elsewhere he claims that even within the Body of Christ, there is no basis for spiritual inferiority. For those members who seem less important or prominent, God compensates to maintain equity in worth, both temporally and eternally.[12]

We care about what other people think. We were created as social creatures, made for relationship. Hence, any notion of complete independence is a myth. We lack the ability to define ourselves in the way we want. Only with serious consequences can I coax myself into believing that I'm the Messiah or some other exalted being so that I can feel good about myself. We define ourselves and achieve some sense of approval through others. However, the opinions of others can be brutal and coercive. Dependence can be an ugly thing along with the abuse that often accompanies it. No one wants to be controlled.

Insofar as we know we have God's approval, we can depend less upon the approval of others. God wants us to free ourselves from this through dependence upon the only Righteous One. Shame makes us run and hide, certain that others feel about us as we feel about ourselves. God's love says, "I love you at your absolute worst. Nothing can separate you from my love, absolutely nothing!"[13] When you're freed from shame, you sing and dance; it doesn't matter who sees you!

But isn't dependence upon God's opinions also coercive? Furthermore, He seems to have more opinions than anyone else! Even the New Testament is filled with a guilt- provoking collection of tedious "do's" and "don'ts." Superficially, this is true! However, God's law is a reflection of His love. In the same way that a mother tells her children not to hurt one another, so too is God's law. Paul writes,

> "Owe nothing to anyone except to love one another; for he who loves his neighbor has fulfilled the law. For this, 'YOU SHALL NOT COMMIT ADULTERY, YOU SHALL NOT MURDER, YOU SHALL NOT STEAL,

YOU SHALL NOT COVET,' and if there is any other commandment, it is summed up in this saying, 'YOU SHALL LOVE YOUR NEIGHBOR AS YOURSELF.' Love does no wrong to a neighbor; love therefore is the fulfillment of the law."[14]

Why does God boss us around? Because He loves us! Why is He punitive? Again, because He loves us! But how can His opinions of us become a foundation for our psychological stability if they depend upon how good we've been? If we've been good, He'll think well of us, if not, we'll shrivel up with guilt! How then can this God be a foundation for our peace?

He'll never take His love from us. We will always be a delight to Him. Yes, we do grieve God and He does consequently chasten us, but we *remain* beloved children. This doesn't change.

In 1969, after dropping out of Berkeley for the second time, I moved to New York and got involved with a therapeutic organization that had come highly recommended. Step #1- they administer a test to you to determine the level of your need. I took the test and it was determined that I needed their services immediately! Step #2- you take their introductory communications course over a weekend. I enrolled immediately.

I found the group highly intimidating. It seemed as if they all had their act together. Smiles never left their faces, and they moved around as if powered by a secret, high-test energy supply. The course was comprised of numerous group exercises, repeating various phrases at command, staring into the eyes of your partner, and other exercises, which I've long forgotten. The other participants seemed to be very excited about what they were doing, and at the completion of the course, they all rushed to sign a paper claiming that their lives had been irreversibly changed by the course. I demurred. One of the leaders asked my why I hadn't signed. "Was I being stubborn?" I asked myself. Why was it that everyone else had derived so much from the course and I hadn't? I knew the reason. I was an "untouchable." Yet I still couldn't sincerely sign their paper.

I explained that I was very willing to sign their paper, but at this particular time, I couldn't affirm what they wanted. However, I was willing to try to apply their techniques to my life, and would return and gladly sign if I found that my life had been irreversibly changed.

However, that didn't seem to be good enough. The leader directed me to go to the third floor and to see a Ms. Bixby (pseudonym, along with the following names). "What's the reason for this," I asked.

"I'm not in a position to explain, but Ms. Bixby will answer you question," she replied.

I went to Bixby's third floor office. It was large and imposing. I knocked at the open door and waited to be addressed. She was busily writing and took her time to lift her head. She didn't have the omnipresent smile of the others.

"Yes?"

"I was instructed to come up to see you," I replied.

"About what?" I explained to her everything that had transpired downstairs.

"Why didn't you sign?" I explained to her that I was quite willing to sign, but I that just needed more time to ascertain whether my life had been changed.

"You'll have to go see Mr. Clark on the fifth floor."

"What's the reason for all of this?" I asked.

"I'm not in a position to explain. I'm just a 'level three' person, but Mr. Clark is a 'level five' person. He can explain." I knocked on the outside of Mr. Clark's fifth floor office. This office was much more imposing and his desk seemed to stretch to the end of the corridor. I waited for Mr. Clark to lift his head. He too didn't have a smile on his face.

"Yes?" I explained that Ms. Bixby had just directed me to see him and related to him the other events.

"Why didn't you sign the paper," he queried with a puzzled look upon his face. I gave him the same exact explanation that I had given Bixby along with my assurances that I was willing to sign.

"You're going to have to see Mr. Matthews on the 15th floor," Clark informed me.

"What is this all about," I asked.

"I can't explain that to you. I'm only a level 'five person', but Mr. Matthews is a 'level seven', and he'll be able to explain to you everything you want to know."

If I remember correctly, I did go to see Matthews, for more of the same. Finally, I left in frustration, bivouacked by the two opposing reactions of intimidation and anger. Despite all of this turmoil, I wanted to return for their next course, convinced that I was just missing the boat that everyone else had successfully boarded. I was only rescued by my failure to raise the money.

Why did I subject myself to such degrading intimidation? Why didn't this undermine their credibility in my eyes? For one thing, I had felt degraded prior to my involvement with this organization and didn't expect any better treatment. Feeling bad about myself was something I had grown up with. To feel an extra measure of degradation wasn't unusual. Although painful, it was normal and didn't require a face-saving response. For another thing, I felt that I was desperately in need of what they had.

God had warned the Israelites to not make treaties with the nations. He would be their defense! He was all they needed. Sometimes we have to humble ourselves before others because of the wrong we have done. At other times, God refuses to let us humble ourselves before any other "powers." He has promised that He will be our Husband and our Provider, and as in a marriage, He will be our Comforter.

We are all degraded, degraded by our sins and self-imposed alienation from the only source of Life. Abraham degraded himself and his wife Sarah. Fearful that he would be killed because Sarah was beautiful and someone would certainly want to take her, Abraham lied, calling Sarah his sister. He degraded them both because he didn't trust God to protect him. King Abimelech subsequently took her to be his wife. However, despite Abraham's faithlessness, God protected him and prevented the King from sleeping with Sarah who was soon to give birth to the child of the "promise," Isaac.

Abraham degraded himself, but God ennobled Abraham. He warned Abimelech in a dream that Sarah was Abraham's wife and that the king must return her immediately. More startling, He informed the king that the coward Abraham was actually a prophet of God and that the king would have to humble himself before this prophet and ask for prayer. "And Abraham prayed unto God, and God healed Abimelech."[15]

In turn, we are to "fear God." Although this might sound primitive or even oppressive, it's real liberty. This phrase means "ultimate concern for the opinion of God." We are either going to be ultimately concerned about the oppressive and arbitrary opinions of humankind or the loving truth of God. Understood in this context, I'd much prefer to be a servant of Truth than of human whim. One degrades while the Other ennobles.

We need not be ashamed around anyone. Paul announces, "He who knew no sin became sin for us all that we might become that righteousness of God in Him."[16] Although it's not yet apparent, we're no longer the degraded bums that we sometimes feel like, but instead the "righteousness of God."

EXERCISE

1. What role have the opinions of others played in your life? How has it adversely affected you?

2. Have you noticed areas where, as you've become more concerned about the opinion of God, you've become less concerned about the opinions of others? In what ways has this been manifested?

3. In what ways has God ennobled you?

---

[1] John 10:1-18

[2] 1 Peter 2:9

[3] Mat. 23:8-12. I don't think that Christ would argue against using these terms as a simple designation of the roles we play. Nor do I think that there is anything wrong with acknowledging "MD" after someone's name. It is important to

communicate that the individual has mastered a certain body of knowledge. However, titles are often used in such a way as to camouflage our true status and obscure the truth that God reveals about the entire human race.

[4] Deut. 17:20

[5] Gal. 3:28

[6] 1 Cor. 7:23

[7] Psalm 8:3-9

[8] Hosea 2:19-20

[9] Eph 5:25-33

[10] 1 Cor. 6:17

[11] 2 Cor. 2:14-16

[12] 1 Cor. 12:24-25

[13] Romans 8:38-39

[14] Rom. 13:8-10

[15] Gen. 20:17

[16] 2 Cor. 5:21

CHAPTER 7

Biblical Expectations

> "These things I have spoken to you, that in
> Me you may have peace. In the world you
> will have tribulation; but be of good cheer, I
> have overcome the world." **John 16:33**

Our expectations largely determine the way we feel about things. Two employees at a large New York firm both received a $1,000 bonus at the end of the year. One was thrilled with the bonus, the other greatly dismayed. The first hadn't expected any bonus; the second had been hoping for at least a $5,000 bonus.

One Muslim scholar writes,

> "A man like this (an unbeliever) will meet with failure in
> all affairs of his life. His moral, civil, and social life, his
> struggle for prosperity and his family life, in short his
> whole life, will be in turmoil. Disorder and confusion will
> be spread on the earth by him. He will, without the least
> reservation, shed blood, violate the rights of others, be
> cruel to them and tyrannize them. By this behavior he will
> create a general atmosphere of disorder and destruction in
> the world. His perverted mind, blurred vision, distorted
> values and evil-generating activities will make life

miserable for both himself and those associated with him."[1]

With such a set of expectations, it should not be a surprise that the West and its very obvious successes represent a serious affront to this understanding of Islam. For Islam to be correct, the West should find itself in moral and physical shambles.

The inevitable clash between our faulty expectations and reality will also discourage the Christian. In my struggle to rise above depression's claws, I became convinced that I needed to receive the "baptism of the Holy Spirit," an empowering by the Spirit, accompanied by the speaking in an unknown language. I was assured that God would readily give this post-salvation gift to the believer who asked in faith. However, as hard as I would try and with as much faith as I could marshal together, I continued to draw a blank. I was told to keep trying and trusting. However, there was also the subtle message that if I failed to receive this gift, it couldn't possibly be God's fault. It therefore would have to be *my* fault.[2]

This expectation tormented me even more than I had been tormented. If I lacked the faith to receive this special gift, then perhaps I also lacked the faith to be saved. This further undermined the little faith that I did have. Fortunately, although I felt like abandoning this demanding God, who likewise had abandoned me, I had nowhere else to turn. In my utter desperation, I continued to trust in Him. Perhaps He would take pity upon me?

I'm far from alone. Many others are battling destructive misconceptions or have left the faith because of them. Many have despaired in being good enough for Christ and have left with their tail stuck between their legs. Some guilt-ridden souls have joined groups like "Religion Anonymous." I'm sure that some have done so without any misunderstanding. They didn't like the idea of a God who called the shots, albeit that He's loving and forgiving. They wanted to call all the shots, whatever the price. For them, "Religion Anonymous" gave them the support they sought to make the break. However, the story was undoubtedly different for others. For them, God had been understood as a demanding task-master looking to crush His faltering subjects. They had suffered grievously under this aberration. Only those who thought their performance far superior and unassailable would want to keep company with such a Deity.

Other despair-provoking misconceptions prevail. The idea is sometimes promoted that salvation must be accompanied by a dramatic confirmatory experience. Some poor deluded souls spend years trying to find this elusive butterfly until they give up in frustration without coming to the assurance that our gracious God receives all who come to Him.[3]

I think it's harder today. Everything we hear heralds the idea that we can find fulfillment in *this* life. The media tantalizes us with portraits of wild romances, exciting vacations, happy lives of comfort and leisure. Modernity has unhinged us from the mediating influences of traditional community and family, in which personal happiness is subordinated to our roles within the clan, and also from traditional religion that placed the expectation of ultimate peace in the afterlife. Today, we've been led to forget about the "after" and to focus upon the "now." The "now" has to provide everything we desire because it's all we have.

We tend to feel a bit defensive when we can't report that our vacation wasn't all it was supposed to be or that we aren't as fulfilled as we should be. This equates to being a failure. This is because our sense of self-worth has become so closely associated with our success at finding fulfillment. "If you're happy, that's all that matters," we hear trumpeted repeatedly. If we're not happy, we feel such pressure to put on a happy mask rather than let people see that we haven't attained.

If social expectations were somewhat different, we might not experience such pressure to attain the unattainable. Happiness is the hardest thing to find when we're looking for it. If only we could derive our sense of well being and fulfillment from something different, perhaps something more basic. Instead we should be respected for having faced the truth about ourselves today. I wish people would say, "Have you discovered something new about yourself today? Have you learned something today that will enable you to more readily laugh at yourself?"

In any event, our expectations have to become more realistic, more in tune with the reality of "God in us." What is this reality? Ultimately God does want us to be happy, but for now, there's a lot of work to be done, and it's going to be arduous.

> "Now no chastening seems to be joyful for the present, but painful; nevertheless, afterward it yields the peaceable fruit of righteousness to those who have been trained by it."[4]

We often fail to realize that we're being trained for the ultimate Olympics. We have an invisible Trainer who has placed us on the perfect regime; He knows exactly how much we can take and often pushes us to the very limits of our endurance.[5] We often awake with chest pains and cramps from the training. However, when we forget that the pain is the result of something necessary and healthful, we panic and fear that we're having an attack of angina. The panic takes us on a downward spiral, and we want to abandon ship. We have to remind ourselves that we're in the hands of the Trainer who loves us and is inflicting this pain out of love. It's so natural that we're going to "groan" in the midst of this training, and as long as we continue to recognize the fact that the "groaning" is part of a process that will make us more agile, we can accept it.[6] The more convinced that we become that every part of the training is necessary, the more enthusiastically we can accept it. And the more we come to see that our primary struggle is against the sin embedded within, the more readily we'll embrace the training. When we loose sight of this perspective, we grow weary and fall to the wayside and need a pep talk.

Of what does this pep talk consist? —Having the right expectations! Besides the reassurance that the process is necessary, temporary, and totally under girded by love, we're reminded that we're not alone. Every one of God's children has to endure the training. Some of the purest saints underwent terrible torment.

> "Still others had trial of mockings and scourgings, yes,

and of chains and imprisonment. They were stoned, they were sawn in two, were tempted, were slain with the sword. They wandered about in sheepskins and goatskins, being destitute, afflicted, tormented— of whom the world was not worthy. They wandered in deserts and mountains, *in* dens and caves of the earth."[7]

These torments might seem very arbitrary and purposeless from our limited perspective. It's hard to accept suffering when we're convinced that there's no purpose for it. Yet we're repeatedly assured that it's all part of God's plan for our lives. He knows exactly what each one of us requires to produce that type of refinement God wants for our lives. Joseph required a certain type of refinement to do the job as the number two man in the land of Egypt. God gave him just the right training. He had Joseph sold as a slave into Egypt where he received much pertinent experience as a manager both in jail and in the household of Potiphar. Moses learned humility during his 40 years of desert exile.

How do we endure such suffering? We all need hope, an expectation that the pain will cease and that, in the long run, we'll emerge into unending joy. Jesus has to be our ultimate example.

"Looking unto Jesus, the author and finisher of *our* faith, who for the joy that was set before Him endured the cross, despising the shame, and has sat down at the right hand of the throne of God. For consider Him who endured such hostility from sinners against Himself, lest you become weary and discouraged in your souls."[8]

Jesus was able to endure because He had placed His expectations and hopes in another realm, one in which they could be satisfied. We could probably endure a day of the most distasteful labor if we know that our labors will be amply rewarded with $10,000. In the same way, if we are convinced that a blissful eternity awaits us, we can better endure the temporary suffering. In the midst of my own despair and depression, had I better understood that brokenness isn't a sign of God's absence or displeasure, but rather His work, I could have better endured.

Our expectations also need their appropriate focus or we'll be confronted with disappointment. What we attain to here is very temporary. The more we place our ultimate hopes upon the temporal, the more we set ourselves up for disappointment and the more prone we become to conflict.[9] Our faith needs to be buried in an unassailable Person. If our faith is attached to circumstances like gaining the respect of the world, we will find ourselves very disappointed.

Buddhism and monistic Hinduism go to an extreme. Desire is the source of suffering. It therefore has to be eliminated. How? Through enlightenment! The Buddhist is taught to see beyond the illusions of this physical world, which promote desire. Hence, the only thing that has value is to transcend this world with its imprisoning desires. This however denies the value of many things we value: family, friends, vocation, and beauty.[10] In contrast, the Christian ideal doesn't eliminate but *subordinates* the things of this world to the value of the next. Yes, the things of this world are very important, but their ultimate fulfillment is found in the next world. Therefore, earth-bound desires and expectations are meaningful and unavoidable. It's good to build a house for your family or to ensure that your children get a good education, but having correct priorities is imperative. Everything finds its ultimate meaning in the context of a relationship with the One who created it all. So there will be disappointments, but these can be minimized as we keep the reality of our relationship with God in perspective.

The Book of Hebrews warns us if we fail to look to Jesus, we'll become weary and discouraged. This is because life can be wearying and depressing. We have to align our expectations with the life of Jesus. He suffered; we'll also suffer; He was rejected and hated; we too will experience this.

Let me anticipate your response: "I already know this. But I feel like I'm too broken to continue on and don't have the level of faith or conviction to sustain me through this ordeal." Let me just reassure you that you're not alone. The One who has promised to never leave nor forsake us is at your side. He knows your pain and weakness and delights in surprising us with His rescue when all hope seems to be gone. At the moment of greatest doubt and failure, the Faithful One appeared to His unfaithful disciples to reassure them that their life was just beginning.

Let me try to anticipate another response: "This Christian life seems so bleak. I need to see the grace of Christ in my life now." You're in good company. All of God's servants reach this point. In many situations, David said that he just couldn't take it any longer, that he would just shrivel up and die without a touch from the Lord.[11] Moses told God he couldn't go on without some divine refreshing. He pushes us to our limits, but this has a very necessary purpose. Only in our utter brokenness can we learn to trust God as we ought.[12]

EXERCISE

1. How have your temporal expectations been unrealistic?

2. What were the costs?

3. How have you learned to biblically adjust your expectations? Has this helped?

---

[1] Towards Understanding Islam, Abul A'la Mawdudi, The Message Publications, pgs. 10-11. Although Christianity also maintains that we "reap what we sow," the Christian message is highly nuanced. For example, see Psalms 37, 73, and the Book of Job.

[2] I later became convinced that this understanding wasn't Scriptural. (Rom. 8:9; Eph. 4:3-6; 1 Cor. 12:13; Col. 2:9-10)

[3] Romans 10:13; John 6:37

[4] Hebrews 12:11

[5] 1 Cor. 10:13

[6] 2 Cor. 5:2

[7] Heb. 11:36-38

[8] Hebrews 12:2-3

[9] James 3:16

[10] Fortunately, most Buddhists do value the things we value, but this is not consistent with the Buddhist philosophy.

[11] Psalm 27:13

[12] 2 Cor. 1:8-10

CHAPTER 8

Do I Have Enough Faith?

"Therefore I say to you, whatever things you ask when you pray, believe that you receive them, and you will have them." **Mark 11:24**

The question of faith fills many of us with apprehension and uncertainty. I had already earned an M.A. and was now in my second seminary struggling with self-doubts. I unwisely unburdened myself to another seminary student about a struggle I was having. He fired back, "Your problem is that you just don't believe," as he hastened away.

I was left bleeding; my foundation was tottering badly. Did I have the minimum level faith needed to get into heaven? I wasn't sure. I didn't know how to answer or how to reassure myself. I could come up with only one answer to my uncertainty. I was going to make a supreme effort to rally every strand of faith I possibly could to carry me across the "finish line" into the "salvation end zone." And I wouldn't confide in anymore seminary students! Then, an even more dismal thought crossed my quaking mind. I'd also have to keep my faith up to the passing level in order to stay saved. Despite all my remedial efforts, doubting my salvation had become a source of the greatest pain and dysfunction.

I can see that I'm not alone in this response. I recently tried to encourage a student to "just trust God." He lamely reassured me, "*I'm* going to trust Him as best *I* can. *I'm* going to try to focus more on Him. *I'm* going to force *myself* to read the Bible." He was almost out of breath as he concluded. I could feel the terrible weight that he had been placing upon his shoulders, a weight no one could bear, and a weigh which I had failed to relieve.

The problem wasn't that he was committing himself to unspiritual disciplines. There's certainly no problem in trusting in God, focusing upon Him, and reading His Word. We should all be doing these things in increasing amounts. Our problem is that we tend to be myopic. We only see the narrow picture at the expense of the grander one. In our failure to trust God, we place our trust upon ourselves and our own efforts. While thinking we're looking at the Eternal, we are really looking at the temporal all over again! "Do *I* have enough faith? Is *it* genuine enough? Is *it* lifting *my* depression? Am *I* spending enough time in prayer? Is *my* prayer emotional enough? Am *I* praying in the right way?" Instead of trusting in God, we are trusting in self to produce and to maintain *our* faith and *our* prayers.

Hopefully, we'll come to despair of not only our faith and prayers, but also of all other efforts and the self-trust we try to manufacture in hope of carrying us into the presence of God. The great British preacher, Charles Spurgeon, declared that he repented even of his prayers.

BUT HOW ARE WE TO ASSURE OURSELVES THAT WE HAVE ENOUGH FAITH?

For one thing, saving faith isn't a matter of quantity. The disciples knew that they didn't have great faith. Jesus wouldn't allow them to think otherwise. It seemed that whenever they'd make some wrong assessment, Jesus would rub their nose in it. The disciples' thinking was left unaffected by the awe-inspiring miracle of feeding thousands with a few loaves and fish. Jesus wouldn't allow their denseness to pass without remark.

"O you of little faith, why do you reason among yourselves

because you have brought no bread? Do you not yet understand, or remember the five loaves of the five thousand and
how many baskets you took up?"[1]

It was plain to them that they needed more faith, and so wisely
they inquired from the very Source, asking Jesus to increase their
faith. In response, Jesus informed them that even the smallest
measure of faith would do. The mustard seed of Jesus' day was the
smallest seed, a mere speck of dust. Jesus insisted that even if our
faith measured up to no more than this, it would be enough to
move trees.[2]

Instead, faith is primarily a matter of focus. Jesus followed this
with a parable about a master and his servant.

> "And which of you, having a servant plowing or tending
> sheep, will say to him when he has come in from the
> field, 'Come at once and sit down to eat'? But will he not
> rather say to him, 'Prepare something for my supper, and
> gird yourself and serve me till I have eaten and drunk, and
> afterward you will eat and drink'? Does he thank that
> servant because he did the things that were commanded
> him? I think not. So likewise you, when you have done all
> those things which you are commanded, say, 'We are
> unprofitable ("unworthy," NIV) servants. We have done
> what was our duty to do.'"[3]

Let me try to modernize this parable. Imagine taking your
fiancée out for a romantic candlelight dinner. The waiter, after
bringing you the main meal, pulls up a chair, sets his own meal
down alongside of yours, and informs the two of you that he's
going to join you. When you protest that your evening plans didn't
include the waiter, he responds, "Didn't I do everything that I was
supposed to do? Didn't I bring you the food you requested? Now I
deserve to join you."

Naturally, you'd protest that even if he performed perfectly, it
still wouldn't entitle him to join the two of you. Jesus tells us that we
should have a similar attitude of mind. Even if we successfully

fulfilled everything that God required of us, we still wouldn't deserve anything from Him. What He gives us, He gives out of love, not out of obligation.[4] He will never allow Himself to be put into such a situation.[5] When we realize that our performance can never obligate God to us, we come to realize the inappropriateness of placing our focus upon self. Not only is this psychologically destructive, it also represents the height of hubris! However unsteady our focus might be, it has to be upon God. There's no way that *my* efforts or faith can get me to the moon, how much less so to heaven!

Shortly after this episode, Jesus told his disciples a parable about two men; one had the proper focus, the other lacked it. The first was consumed by a self-focus. His trust was in himself and not in God. Consequently, his prayer was a form of auto-stimulation, for his own self-edification, and not a communication with God. He prayed "with himself."

> "Also He spoke this parable to some who *trusted in themselves* that they were righteous, and despised others: "Two men went up to the temple to pray, one a Pharisee and the other a tax collector. The Pharisee stood and prayed thus *with himself*, 'God, I thank You that I am not like other men—extortioners, unjust, adulterers, or even as this tax collector.'"[6]

A faith that trusts in self not only fails to be acknowledged by God, it also has to justify itself by looking down upon others. By foolishly trusting in self against the pleadings of our conscience, we try to find external affirmation. This affirmation often comes in the form of degrading others while promoting ourselves through an external practice of righteousness.

The Pharisees were known to perform righteously in the public to win public approval. In effect, this Pharisee prayed, "I'm more worthy than others. This makes me deserving of Your blessings." The Pharisee's prayer was nothing more than a self-promoting speech to a non-existent audience.

At a distance from the Pharisee, a degraded sinner cried a desperate prayer. In his shame, he couldn't even look up to heaven.

From all indications, he had little expectation of being heard by God. His faith was anything but great. However, he had one advantage over the Pharisee; he had despaired of himself. He knew that he couldn't handle his problems; his focus had already turned from expecting anything of substance from himself. His trust, however shaky, had to be placed elsewhere. With his focus wavering, he turned to his last resort, "God have mercy upon me, a sinner."[7] He had little faith, but the faith he did have could only look towards God. Jesus tells us that it was this sinner who had left the Temple forgiven and embraced.

Ultimately, it's not about the quantity or even so much about the quality of our faith. Ultimately, it's about the Object of our faith. Are we placing our faith in Jesus or in ourselves? If we have despaired of self and are looking at Jesus as a last resort, then we are excellent candidates for faith. Hebrews reads, "By faith they (Israel) passed through the Red Sea."[8] However, we know that their faith wasn't stellar. Just prior to God splitting the sea, their faith failed them.

> "Then they said to Moses, 'Because there were no graves in Egypt, have you taken us away to die in the wilderness? Why have you so dealt with us, to bring us up out of Egypt? Is this not the word that we told you in Egypt, saying, 'Let us alone that we may serve the Egyptians?' For it would have been better for us to serve the Egyptians than that we should die in the wilderness.'"[9]

How do we understand the discrepancy? How can they both have faith but not have faith according to the Exodus account? It seems that both quantitatively and qualitatively Israel was faith-deficient. However, they were between a rock and a hard place. Deliverance demanded that they pass through the midst of the sea to safety. Their focus couldn't possibly be upon themselves, nor even upon Moses. However little faith they had, it could only be directed towards God. Only He could keep back those terrifying walls of water. The only path of safety was through the water; the only hope was God.

He set up the scenario in which Israel would have to trust in Him. God also does this for us. He pulls away our crutch by taking us out of Egypt and leads us through a dreadful sea. With the threatening seas of depression piled up on either side of us, we are mercifully left with no choice but to look to Him alone. How much faith do we need? It doesn't matter! It's not a matter of how much, but rather "to Whom."

ONE LAST CONCERN:

What about doubt? Concerns about the purity of our faith plague us. Doesn't the presence of doubt suggest that such a faith isn't adequate for a relationship with God? With this in question, how can we adore a God who'll disqualify us if we fail to rid ourselves of doubt? We'll slide down the slippery slope of self-obsession.

The answer is threefold. Firstly, if we have unrepented sin, doubt is a healthy response. It should lead us to repentance as pain should lead us to withdraw our hand from a hot stove. How joyous then the restoration![10]

Secondly, there are the many examples of saints with unsteady faith upon whom God had placed His eternal love. Besides the examples of those mentioned above, there are even examples of those who *refused* to believe. God would first have to submit to *their* demands! There was Thomas who had his specifications. He refused to believe despite hearing the reports from many of the disciples that Jesus had risen. He had also heard this very testimony from the mouth of Jesus Himself. He wasn't going to believe unless Christ would appear to him so that he could put his fingers through the holes in his hands and his hand into Jesus' pierced side.[11] Who was he that he could demand to intrude so intimately, so intrusively upon the suffering of the Savior? It would have been somewhat more fitting if he had merely demanded to see the Savior rather than to finger Him as if He were a mere side of beef. Nevertheless, Jesus condescended to Thomas' demands.

Here's the point— if Jesus is willing to humble Himself to

fulfill such inappropriate demands, how much more so is He ready to come to the aid of His people who cry out to Him, "Lord, help my unbelief!"

This brings me to my final point. If we have any idea of the extent of love that our Suffering Savior has for us, these fears would melt away. I don't understand that love. I can't! Paul tells us that His love goes beyond anything we can fathom. It's a love that even transcends anything we can ask for.[12] Whatever you might imagine this love to be, it's far greater.

In view of such a love, our weaknesses, doubts, and failures don't constitute a barrier to the grace of God. Instead they have become the very gateway to blessing.[13]

EXERCISE:

1. What doubts have you had about the quantity or quality of your faith?

2. How did these doubts affect you?

3. How would it make you feel if you believed that God was ten times more loving than you had previously imagined? Would this help you to accept you doubts and failings?

---

[1] Matthew 16:8-9

[2] Luke 17:6

[3] Luke 17:7-10

[4] Each of us is miles away from fulfilling our duty! (James 3:2)

[5] Romans 11:35

[6] Luke 18:9-11

[7] Luke 18:13

[8] Hebrews 11:29

[9] Exodus 14:11-12

[10] Luke 15:22-24
[11] John 20:25
[12] Eph. 3:18-20
[13] 2 Cor. 12:9-10

CHAPTER 9

Achieving Integration

"For I say, through the grace given to me, to everyone who is among you, not to think of himself more highly than he ought to think, but to think soberly, as God has dealt to each one a measure of faith." **Romans 12:3**

Sober thinking is essential. If we regard ourselves wrongly, we'll make unwise and costly decisions. My church was putting on a musical. The leading role was of course Jesus, and I wanted to play Jesus. Not that I had had much experience at this, and I certainly lacked the skills, but there were several young and attractive women in the pews, and I wanted to look good in their eyes. I didn't know how to read music, but no matter, I'd learn. I just felt strongly in my heart that I could do it. Years of inflating myself in my own eyes were about to lead me into humiliation and depression's deepest dungeon. By God's grace and a degree of discernment on the part of the director, I didn't get that role nor any other major role. Mercifully, I was spared!

This raises the question, "How can we gain the wisdom necessary to make wise decisions?" Firstly, this depends upon seeing ourselves clearly enough. But this is more easily said than done. We have an unconscious dumping ground. Into it we throw all of our undesirable experiences and the parts of ourselves that we don't like, anything that threatens our sense of significance. As a result of our mental gymnastics, we suffer from a self-imposed blindness. Although ignorance can be bliss, it usually doesn't serve us very well. Truly, it's anxiety provoking to be driving on the highway and to find the gas gauge on "empty." It might temporarily quiet the anxiety to forget about the gas gauge, but it will later return as a roaring lion. Likewise, those buried parts continue to resurface at the least opportune times. We may say that we want to come to some self-acceptance and to bring all of those rejected parts into the light, but we really don't want this.

For clarity sake, I must make a sharp distinction between "self-acceptance" and what we generally think of as "self-esteem." They are diametrically opposed. Self-acceptance is about accepting yourself the way you really are, warts and all. It doesn't mean that you have to like everything about yourself— no one should! If we're honest with ourselves, there are many things we would love to change. Instead, self-acceptance is a necessary precondition to seeing ourselves exactly the way we are. Failure to *accept* self translates into an unwillingness to *see* self. When we accurately see self, we have at our disposal the data upon which decision-making depends. This is a precondition for wise management.

When we think of our self-estimation, we usually think of it in terms of *building* our self-esteem. While self-acceptance aims at arriving at the truth about ourselves, self-esteem aims at feeling good about ourselves without much consideration of whether or not this estimation is a true one.

There is nothing wrong about feeling good about oneself. We all want this. However, it becomes a question of the price that we pay for this feeling. If it is at the expense of truth, then the price is too high. Living in darkness exacts a high price in the long run. Because I wouldn't face the truth about myself in terms of my musical ability, I would have paid a very high price for my delusion. Contrary to common opinion on the subject, recent studies have shown that high scores in self-esteem do not correlate well with either high performance or positive social behavior.[1]

The reason we don't accept ourselves the way we are is very simple. It's just too painful! The human dilemma is this: we have at least two selves! One I will call the "Idealized Self" (IS). This is the self with which we feel comfortable, the self we like to present to the world. This is the self we see as lovable, desirable, competent, respectable, and virtuous. When we feel that others see us in light of our IS, we feel secure and respected. We feel comfortable with others and at times, even expansive. In order to keep the IS façade in place, we surround ourselves with people who see us in light of our IS and pursue experiences that will affirm our belief in the reality of our IS. When we're established in our belief of the correctness of our IS, we feel secure and are willing to venture forth.

As the bipolar sufferer swings from manic into the depressed state, so too will we eventually swing into our "Rejected Self" (RS). This is the part of ourselves we see as unlovable, unworthy, and incapable. We feel ashamed of this self and understandably want to hide it from others. When we feel that others see us in this light, we feel insecure and vulnerable and want to run away. We're thankful for those who will love us in the midst of our RS but fear that eventually they'll tire of us, and sometimes they do.

We'll do anything to banish this unwanted ogre back into the pits of the subconscious and to resurrect the IS. Depending upon our personality, we have various methods to accomplish this feat. Some can accomplish this very easily by merely pushing a switch. In an interview, Ted Bundy, the serial killer, explained how he could dissociate himself from his actions in a flash. Such people have a harder time achieving integration. We all receive a pay-off when we dissociate from painful thoughts, but some are better at it than others.

Most of us don't have the facility of a Ted Bundy, but most of us haven't progressed to become serial killers either. There's a great price to be paid for dissociation, and it gets greater the more skilled we become at it.

Not having that ready switch, we have to engage in more rigorous efforts to banish the RS. Some of us achieve some sense of well-being by spending money; others regain their IS by saving money. For most of us, securing achievement, beauty, recognition, power, or popularity are the usual tactics, but we find that we always need more of it to retain the peace of the IS. John D. Rockefeller was once asked, "How much more money will it take to finally satisfy you?" He answered, "Always a little bit more."

Whether he actually said this or not is unimportant, because we know this to be true for ourselves. How many times have we thought to ourselves, "If I only had that woman or that man or that job or that house or that promotion, I would be happy!" Inevitably, we've found that the happiness would only last for a week or two and sometimes only for an hour. Then we'd find ourselves hunting for a stronger fix to build the IS even higher.

Often times, psychotherapy merely plays along with our malignant script of retaining and building our IS. Therapists go to "Building Self-Esteem" seminars; they seek ways of helping their clients achieve successes; they reassure the clients that the IS is the *real* self. Myopically, many assume that whatever brings the client happiness and peace in the short run should be the goal of therapy. From the above perspective, they are merely *enabling* a dysfunctional system. The client continues to swing between the IS and RS at the expense of developing a consistent, unified, and integrated perspective. The psychotherapist readily climbs into our dysfunctional cycle to enable us to retain the delusions to keep our crumbling facade in one piece. How much healthier and more in accord with reality to face and accept our RS! If we can learn to accept ourselves, warts and all, we can break our addiction to those things we so desperately need to maintain our IS, the popularity, success, etc. We have to learn to laugh at ourselves! Liberation is self-laughter.

Very few of us perceive that we live in a world of delusion. This is part of the delusion itself. As improbable as this might sound, Shelley Taylor believes that the evidence for this is unassailable:

> "People are positively biased in their assessment of themselves and of their ability to control what goes on around them...The widespread existence of these biases and the

ease by which they can be documented suggests that they are normal."[2]

"Instead of an awareness and acceptance of both positive and negative elements of their personalities, most people show a keen awareness of their positive qualities and attributes, an extreme estimation of their ability to master the environment...Not only are these assessments positive, they appear to be unrealistically so. It is not just that people believe they are good, but they think they are better than reality can sustain."[3]

Finding this type of self-delusional thinking to be ubiquitous among the "healthy" while finding more accurate thinking among the depressed, Dr. Taylor had concluded that these illusions are actually "positive" and necessary to healthy functioning. This represents a radical departure from what had traditionally been regarded as sound mental health—the accurate perception of reality. Are these really the only two choices—delusion or depression? Is it possible to accurately see life and not be depressed about ourselves? Do we require rose-colored glasses, at least when we try to perceive ourselves?

Therapists who understand that truth and self-acceptance must be foundational often despair of enlightening their clients. They understand that the vast number of clients come to them not because they want to know themselves better, but because they want to feel better about themselves. This also pertains to people who have great attainments, who are at the tops of their fields. We might think that those who have a strengthened IS would be impregnable to the disparaging messages of their RS and feelings of insecurity, but this isn't the case. Whatever is suppressed will bounce back like a submerged, inflated ball, however prominent our IS.

Robert B. Millman, a professor of psychiatry at Cornell Medical School and a psychotherapist for numerous celebrities, has come to recognize that those people who are particularly successful at elevating their IS, through their successes and the adoration of others, show signs of what Millman calls "acquired narcissism" characterized by depression, poor judgment, and poor parenting skills.

"When a billionaire or a celebrity walks into the room, everyone looks at him. He's a prince. He has the power to change your life, and everybody is very conscious of that...Because they truly don't believe that the world is real, they begin to think they're invulnerable. Some even risk their lives, since the world can't hurt them if it's not real."[4]

The price of not achieving true self-acceptance is living a dangerous delusion. The celebrity is no different than we are. They've just been more successful at elevating themselves and at living a fantasy, something that we're all trying to do.

Millman was asked how he treats his clients. Although he tries to inject some reality into their lives, he acknowledged that too much honest feedback would drive them away.

NEGATIVE CONSEQUENCES

Failing to accept ourselves and living in unreality have many negative consequences. Insofar as we fail to see and understand ourselves, we'll fail to understand the world around us. If we're unwilling to accept the dark side, we'll resent others who try to hold the mirror up to us. Furthermore, we'll be unwilling to accept their dark side. It should not be surprising that if we're unaccepting of our faults, we'll not be accepting of others' faults. This will repeatedly occur with those with whom we are closest. Problems need to be dealt with, and a mature and healthy relationship is built upon truth and openness. Our loved ones see both our IS and RS and understandably will find certain aspects of both upsetting. Many couples can't work out their differences because at least one party doesn't want to see the blemishes and will resist such an exposure. As a result, while defensiveness is ubiquitous, an apology will be hard to find.

Harmony will also be threatened by the fact that if my IS is largely inflated, I'm not going to be content with any partner who does not occupy my inflated station in life. A "quality" person is only going to be satisfied with another "quality" person. What happens when the one "quality" person awakes to realize that his spouse is no longer his equal?

If we don't understand ourselves, we can't understand others. The idealized world that I had created for myself became the lens through which I viewed reality. I was always depressed, but when I fell into a major depression and had only my RS to keep me company, a deep confusion and pain set in. Part of my confusion was the product of having two lenses perceiving life in completely different ways. Through one lens I looked down upon others; through the other, I was utterly intimidated by them. This confusion just intensified the pain. If only I had had some perspective, some oversight of the problem, I might have been able to form some strategy, but I found myself wrestling in complete darkness. I didn't have a clue about the foe nor about his designs. Unable to see reality correctly and consistently, I fell into unproductive obsessions. I so desperately craved hope, but hope often rests upon the shoulders of a hopeful strategy, and a hopeful strategy upon understanding— something unreachable from the grasp of depressions' obsessions.

Fighting from within the IS-RS cycle has other major costs. One obvious one is our efforts at image management. It requires a lot of energy and self-focus. Just look at all the time we spend grooming ourselves, the care we put into selecting our clothing, our choice of words, our obsessing over what we had said, the choosing of people and things with which we want to associate. It's a daunting and costly operation. Granted, we'll never see the end of this occupation in the span of this life, but it can be minimized.

Along with our self-obsessions, we obsessively compare ourselves to others. It goes with the turf. When maintaining our IS becomes our prime concern, we condemn ourselves to obsessively scrutinize others lest they exceed our performance or recognition quota.

It's always comparative. If we move to a poor country where our income exceeds that of everyone else, it feels very different than if we lived among millionaires. What had satisfied before no longer satisfies. This too is the case with our performance demands. Self-worth requires performance to confirm the IS. If our performance falls below the prevailing standards, the IS will become increasingly difficult to maintain.

ACHIEVING SELF-ACCEPTANCE

Many from all schools of thought have come to see the failings of trying to base our welfare upon our IS. Even if we're performing well, the RS is sure to return along with everything else we've banished into our unconscious. The attempt to merely detach ourselves from this reality of strife and striving through some form of discipline or meditation fails to appreciate the strength of the glue that keeps us stuck in our mental rut.

Some have sought their nirvana through relationships. However, their inflated expectations have placed undue pressure upon these relationships. No one would ever be able to fit the bill of a virtual love machine spitting out "unconditional positive regard" day and night. We all have our needs and limits. The best way to scare potential friends away is to show them that you have inflated expectations for them to fulfill. They may flatter themselves for a while with the idea that they can become that type of savior, but eventually, reality will set in. Making a god out of a friend is the surest way to see their clay feet. We have to learn to love the other, warts and all, as the other learns to love us despite ourselves.

Others have put their hope in a loving group or family. John Bradshaw, a psychologist and a proponent of the Recovery Movement, claims that because our dysfunctional, over-critical families have instilled us with a shame-based mentality, we need a loving family to correct this deficiency. We can outgrow the shame once we receive the love that we had never received.

Although I believe that Bradshaw is correct in recognizing and eschewing the self-defeating pressures we place upon ourselves, I doubt that this kind of love can do the trick. Firstly the above critique of relationships also pertains to groups. Secondly, doesn't this place undue trust upon a group and its members? They may be as dysfunctional as we are. Are they any more capable of true love than us?

Thirdly, wouldn't this promote an unhealthy dependence upon a group? Wouldn't such dependence increase the possibility of sickness and abuse? What happens when the membership changes? When new people more lovable than myself enter the group? What happens when I feel that I must take a stand against the group consensus? Won't I be risking the very foundation my life rests upon? What happens when the sentiments of the group change? Must I always change along with the group?

Lastly, isn't this merely substituting one drug for another, putting in the place of God a mere group of fickle humans like myself? What type of foundation will a group provide? Will this group continue to love and forgive me even as I continue to fall back into drugs for many years? How much better to have a foundation consisting of unchanging love, perfect wisdom, unending patience, and unlimited power!

We require a Foundation that will bear with us no matter how ugly we are, no matter how many times we fall, no matter how many times we betray our Foundation. We need a Foundation whose love is not a self-centered love and isn't fabricated for the purpose of moving Person X from point "A" to point "B."

Paul writes about this transcendent Love who has embraced us to Himself forever: "I have been crucified with Christ; it is no longer I who live but Christ lives in me; and the life I live in the flesh, I live by faith in the Son of God, who loved me and gave Himself for me."[5] Therefore, it's no longer so important who I am, but who He is. He knows me perfectly, and despite the ugliness He sees, He loves me intensely and permanently.

Knowing this, I can laugh at everything else, even at myself. My failures are no longer as big as they had been. My weaknesses are all surmountable and have even become sources of great blessing, because He nurtures and comforts us in our weakness.[6]

These assurances give me courage. I can begin to even risk seeing myself. It isn't pleasant; it never is, but its fruits are undeniable. I'm no longer trying to be the lead in my church's musical. OK, I am married now; it's easier for me; I no longer have to impress the single gal. Yes, defeats and rejections still hurt, but I no longer need to compensate for them through self-delusion. I can face the light because of the One who suffers along with me.[7]

Depression's jaws no longer lurk in an unfathomable darkness. God has created light by which I can now wrap my eyes around both selves. I can accept both, because He does. That doesn't mean that I like everything I see. There are some attitudes and behaviors that simply must go. This is something my wife applauds. A failure to accept self is a failure to take criticism and responsibility. It's a refusal to change. If our entire value as a person and security rest upon seeing ourselves in a certain light and through a certain lens, anyone who tampers with our "light" will be met with sharp resistance. Self-acceptance provides an open door to correction and to a willingness to change.

EXERCISE: The Titanic was a sturdy ship but pride led its promoters to elevate it to the status of invincibility. We know the consequences of this misjudgment.

1. In what ways have you misjudged yourself? What were the consequences?

2. Are you able to identify the causes of your misjudgment? What are they?

3. Have you been able to successfully address these undying causes? How? What have been the results?

4. How has a relationship with God enabled you to face the truth about yourself?

[1] "Deflating Self-Esteem's Role in Society's Ills," Erica Goode, New York Times, Oct. 1, 2002.

[2] Positive Illusion, Shelley E. Taylor, Basic Books, NY, NY, p. 46.

[3] Ibid. pg. 43.

[4] "Acquired Situational Narcissism," Robert B. Millman, New York Times Magazine, 12/9/01, pg. 50.

[5] Gal. 2:20

[6] 2 Cor. 12:9-10

[7] Heb. 4:15

CHAPTER 10

The IS Deflator: Psalm 15

"Who may worship in your sanctuary, Lord?
Who may enter your presence on your holy
hill? Those who lead blameless lives and do
what is right, speaking the truth from sincere
hearts. Those who refuse to slander others or
harm their neighbors or speak evil of their
friends. Those who despise persistent sinners,
and honor the faithful followers of the Lord
and keep their promises even when it hurts.
Those who do not charge interest on the
money they lend, and who refuse to accept
bribes to testify against the innocent. Such
people will stand firm forever."

This can be a disturbing Psalm. I'd love to examine people's
brain waves as they read various portions of Scripture. I'm
sure that I'd find a flurry of brain activity as they read Psalm 15.
This is because this Psalm presents us with impossibly high standards of salvation. To enter into God's presence, to have a saving
relationship with Him, we need to live *"blamelessly"* and to speak
the truth "from sincere hearts." Who among us has always lived
blamelessly, always speaking truth from a sincere heart? For one

thing, our hearts are seldom if ever completely sincere. We find ourselves engaging in "image management" even in regards to our own perceptions of self. We're slow to take responsibility for our wrongs. We try to justify ourselves by convincing ourselves that we hadn't done wrongly. Only in time, do we come to accept the Spirit's verdict of "guilty" instead of our own acquittal.

Feeling vulnerable and inadequate isn't fun, but exorcizing Psalm 15 from the Bible is no answer. Psalm 15 can be replaced with hundreds of other verses to billy-stick us into the dust. Try this one on for size:

> "Do nothing from selfishness or empty conceit, but with humility of mind regard one another as more important than yourselves; do not merely look out for your own personal interests, but also for the interests of others."[1]

These verses seem to call our entire hope of righteousness and salvation is called into question. If we haven't met the standards, we can forget about entering into God's presence, at least that's the way it appears! In defending ourselves against these terrifying charges of sin, there are three usual responses. We can punish ourselves, repress the charge, or convince ourselves we're not guilty as charged.

Self-punishment is usually followed by a resolution to try harder and do better. However, no matter how strenuous our resolve, we continue to fail. It's just not humanly possible to be blameless in this life.[2] Sin is always present, and it's always battling against our best intentions.[3]

Repression doesn't work much better. We can't keep running from the commands of Scripture. We encounter them on every page of the Bible, and in the New Testament, they even seem to become more demanding.[4] Nor can we avoid the commands by avoiding Scripture; they're also written upon our heart.

A more common response is re-interpretation. Here we merely re-interpret Scripture to prove our innocence, even our superiority and worthiness. This is Pharisaic. No longer do we have to be blameless, just *relatively* blameless compared to others. We no longer have to be like Jesus as long as we're trying.[5] We convince ourselves that Jesus' commands aren't really that demanding, that it's obvious that Jesus doesn't want us to feel guilty and depressed. Therefore, He'd never require such impossibly high standards.

In my course on depression and despair, I require my students to make daily journal entries based upon the reading of a Psalm. I've been taking note of their responses to Psalm 15. While some take the Psalm as a positive encouragement to try harder, most are clearly wounded by it. I imagine that I can even hear their groans as they struggle with it. Some cry out in their journals, "Lord, help me."

If we're honest with ourselves, this has to be our response. We've been brought to destitution, despairing of ever being able to attain the requirements of eternal life. We've "tried harder" and have repeatedly despaired of making the grade. All we can honestly say is "Lord, have mercy upon me, a sinner."

However, this is exactly the state of mind that we're supposed to have. Paul declares that this is exactly what God has planned.

> "But the Scripture has confined all under sin, that the promise by faith in Jesus Christ might be given to those who believe."[6]

Scripture must first break us before it will mend us. We first must be humbled before we can be exalted. Scripture must first show us the impossibility of relying upon self to scale the "holy mountain" of God before it applies the holy balm to our hearts. Self-despair must precede encouragement in the same way that awareness of sin must precede forgiveness. If you forgive someone who has no knowledge that he's wronged you in some way, he'll resent your insinuation that he had done something wrong to you. However, if he has already come to the awareness that he's done you a terrible wrong and is feeling guilty about it, your forgiveness becomes the very balm he's hoping for. This is the prime purpose of the Law:

> "But before faith came, we were kept in custody under the law, being shut up to the faith which was later to be

revealed. Therefore the Law has become our tutor *to lead us* (emphasis mine) to Christ, so that we may be justified by faith."[7]

When we understand our hopeless condition along with our inability to rectify it, the gift of His Son and His Righteousness becomes so healing. This is how law leads us to mercy. The law condemns and relegates us to hopelessness and despair to prepare us to see the Savior. We come to see that the Cross possesses unimaginable love in reaching down to failures so utterly unworthy of Him. We come to embrace the fact that it's no longer about our righteousness and performance but His alone! Paul repeatedly affirms the fact that if we have Jesus, we have everything we need.

"But by His doing you are in Christ Jesus, who became to us wisdom from God, and righteousness and sanctification, and redemption."[8]

From this perspective, the commands of God are beautiful and precious.[9] One student responded to Psalm 15 by praising God for His Law in that it showcased the grace of Jesus Christ poignantly. While Psalm 15 was telling her she was condemned, Christ was crying out even more loudly, "I have overcome by taking on the condemnation for you." For her, the Law was a constant reminder of her failures and lack of any worthiness. Correspondingly, it was also a constant and vivid reminder of the gift of Jesus Christ.

Instead of fleeing from its murderous grip, the Law is now a vehicle by which we can praise our Savior for delivering us to a necessary righteousness that we could never attain on our own. The Law, which had once so viciously stripped us of any hope, has now become a proclamation of our ultimate safety in Jesus. Embracing our safety, we can now also embrace the commands of the Law to perform them not out of fear of perdition, but in thankfulness of redemption from our perdition.

So often had I set out from home to teach with a sense of condemnation gnawing at my heart like a borer worm. I struggled against the demonic accusation that I wasn't worthy to teach. Often, I tried to retaliate by convincing myself that I was worthy or I'd try to run from the accusation until it lassoed my mental apparatus with a grip that wouldn't relent. "How can you teach others when you're still struggling yourself. Look at your motives! Are you trying to call them spiritual? Look at your faith! Are you trying to say that you're without doubts? Just look at you! How much love do you have for others? You're so consumed with yourself!"

Often, I felt so intimidated by the accusations that I wanted to call my school and to tell them to find someone else. I hadn't understood the extent of the grace of God. I hadn't fully embraced the truth that we have the righteousness of Christ Himself, that our sins had been washed away, that it is no longer I who live but Christ within me. When I came to understand this more fully, I learned a new response to the accusations. "Devil, you tell me that I'm not worthy. You are so right. I'm not worthy, but I have a God who is so entirely worthy, who has given me His own Righteousness. I have His very life within me, and it's by this life, and not by my own, that I stand."

This understanding has been so freeing. I'm no longer intimidated by these accusations. Instead, I revel in them! They remind me from where I've come and cause me to rejoice all the more in Jesus and His Righteousness.

BUT DOESN'T PSALM 15 ALSO PROVIDE US WITH A MORAL MANDATE?

Yes, it does! We are supposed to strive to obediently imitate Christ. However, if our motivation isn't flowing forth from an understanding that we are forever beloved children of God through Christ, we'll find ourselves striving either out of fear and guilt or out of self-righteousness. Both approaches serve to minimize faith in God at the price of obsession upon self. If we're not confident of God's assurances of His everlasting love, then we'll turn to self for those assurances.

If obedience isn't first built upon a foundation of faith and gratitude, it will rest upon the crippling notion that it's about our own performance. However, if we approach Psalm 15 with the assurance that God has lovingly provided for all of our needs, then we can approach it with joy, knowing what a privilege it is to serve God.[10]

Obedience is the result of the gift, not the cause of it. We often feel more comfortable with *earning* than with humbly receiving. Jacob had felt this way. Even though he had connived for so much he had received, he never liked the feeling of merely receiving a free gift. After pulling the wool over his father Isaac's eyes and cheating his brother Esau out of his birthright, he fled for his life from the wrath of Esau. On the way to his uncle Laban in Padan Aram, he had a curious encounter. In a dream, God *promised* Jacob that He'd graciously and unconditionally give him everything that He'd promised to Abraham. After he awoke, knowing that this had been a message from God, Jacob ungraciously turned the gracious promise into a business transaction:

> "Then Jacob made a vow, saying, '*If* (emphasis mine) God will be with me and will keep me on this journey that I take, and will give me food to eat and garments to wear, and I return to my father's house in safety, then the Lord will be my God...and of all that You give me I will surely give a tenth to You.'"[11]

Jacob had not yet learned how destitute of hope he was. He hadn't yet understood that he had to receive like a little baby who couldn't offer anything for his keep other than a belch and a dirty diaper. He was in no position to earn anything from God. God didn't require his "tenth." The law hadn't yet exercised its full effect over his proud psyche.

A DIFFERENT EXAMPLE: ANGER

I have a problem with anger. It's not that anger in itself is a bad thing. It can mobilize our thinking against injustice and empower us to deal with problems. Jesus became angry, and He expressed the anger righteously. My problem is that I don't always harness the anger for righteous purposes. I use it within my own heart to punish people.

My two younger brothers don't seem to struggle with it the way I do. Perhaps it's my genetic inheritance that makes anger into an unruly force. Perhaps it was my position in my family as firstborn, or perhaps it was my own early choices to implement anger that made it more deeply entrenched. I haven't been able to figure that one out, but I do know that there's something appealing about anger. It empowers and puts you in the driver's seat. You become the righteous judge. Even now, I recognize that there's a part of me that likes getting angry even when it's not appropriate and goes against my faith. This is because anger is a persuasive prosecutor. It's always convinced that it's in the right and makes a good case for it, at least for a while.

However, I also know that when used improperly, it exacts a tremendous price, far more than it's worth. It disrupts my peace with God. I know what pleases God and when I go against it, I find myself in turmoil. Anger has to be used righteously, to correct bad situations and to extend corrective grace to the wrongdoer. However, when I harbor bitterness and unforgiveness, righteousness isn't being served. In fact, it violates several cardinal truths. I have to treat others as God has treated me. He's forgiven me and has received me. This becomes a mandate for me. Furthermore, there are many hurts that we just have to absorb without revenging ourselves in our hearts upon the perpetrators. If I don't get the promotion or raise I feel I deserve, I have to accept it as God's will. God is omniscient and omnipotent. That means that only what He allows can come into my life. The fact that a trial has come into my life means that He has allowed it in order to accomplish His blessed purposes in my life.

After the death of their father Jacob, Joseph's brothers were fearful that Joseph would now take revenge upon them. They had wanted to kill him but instead sold him as a slave into Egypt. There, Joseph languished as a slave and a prisoner for about 17 years.

However, Joseph explained to them that although what they had done was wrong, it was also part of God's glorious plan.

> "As for you, you meant evil against me, but God meant it for good in order to bring about this present result, to preserve many people alive."[12]

It follows, that if God is using everything that comes into our lives to accomplish His gracious plan for us,[13] we aren't justified in holding on to bitterness and unforgiveness. It would be tantamount to saying, "God, I don't believe that the hurt done to me has any redeeming purpose. What happened to me just shouldn't have happened. I'm so sure of that, that I going to play judge and executioner." It also affirms that I'm in the morally superior position that I can play judge. This is a denial of the Gospel, as if to tell God, "I know enough and am pure enough that I can pass judgment upon others without any worry that I myself might be guilty of similar things, thereby incurring Your judgment. I possess a superior righteousness, my own, which has placed me in a position where I can pass judgment. I'm not guilty; I don't require forgiveness!"

In this trial, the demonic accusations are reversed. Instead of being unworthy, our "victimization" has made us more worthy than others. The accusation is against those who've caused hurt. "They've humiliated you and ruined your life! You could have been happy and had what you deserved. How can you allow them to get away with this? They should be punished!"

It's a blessing that we experience divine chastening when we assume such faithless attitudes. The chastening strips us and causes us to reexamine the implications of the Gospel. With the prompting of the Spirit through His Word, we can begin to see how our attitudes have missed the mark of truth, and we begin to talk to ourselves about this. Consequently, I've been learning how to preach a sermon to myself in this area. "Devil, I can't maintain bitterness. How can I when it's all part of God's gracious plan? He knows exactly what I need, and this is part of it. Everything He brings into my life, He uses for good. How can I not be content with such a God? How can I complain against Him by being discontent with my life? How can I not forgive others when He has been so gracious with me, when I deserve absolutely nothing from Him?"

How does this relate to depression? I've consistently found that as I've followed His truth, I've found some measure of peace. For years, I tried to find that peace through understanding or cathartically re-experiencing my past. It's never paid any dividends. It's just turned me aside from more fruitful areas. I don't exactly know why I have more of a problem with anger than do my brothers, but it doesn't seem to matter. However, it is important that I understand some other things.

1. My anger doesn't conform to the specifications of Scripture.
2. It doesn't accomplish anything good for me or for others (James 1:19-20).
3. It cheats me of God's peace and denies the foundation of my hope—the Gospel.
4. I need to be aware of its dynamics: what triggers and inflames it.
5. I need to know how to counteract it and to preach truth to myself.
6. I need to learn how to use it constructively.

Let me suggest a model prayer that might be of help: *"Lord, help me to see my unworthiness, my failures, my lies, my sinful efforts to reinterpret Scripture to suit myself. Cause me to despair of myself and my efforts to justify myself and to convince myself of my own righteousness. Open my eyes to the extent of Your mercy that I might come to trust in You completely and to adore You for all you've done for me, and cause me to be content with Your daily bread."*

EXERCISE:

1. How do you respond to the commands of God? Is it based

upon the knowledge of grace?

2. With which accusations do you struggle?

3. How might the comfort of the Gospel address these accusations?

4. Understanding the Gospel, what sermons might you preach to yourself?

---

[1] Phil. 2:3-4

[2] Rom. 3:19-20; 1 John 1:8

[3] Gal. 5:17

[4] Mat. 5-7. Here's an example: "You have heard that it was said, 'You shall not commit adultery'; but I say to you that everyone who looks at a woman with lust for her has already committed adultery with her in his heart." Matthew 5:27-28

[5] 1 Peter 1:15-16

[6] Gal. 3:22

[7] Gal. 3:23-24

[8] 1 Cor. 1:30

[9] Rom. 7:12

[10] John 4:34

[11] Gen. 28:20-22

[12] Gen. 50:20

[13] Eph. 2:10; Rom. 8:28; Psalm 23

CHAPTER 11

Assured of God's Love

And as Moses lifted up the serpent in the wilderness, even so must the Son of Man be lifted up, that whoever believes in Him should not perish but have eternal life. **John 3:14-15**

Where we lack this assurance, we also lack trust. We can't trust or love God if we're not certain that He receives and loves us. If we can't trust God, then by default we'll have to trust in self with all the obsessive bondage that goes along with it. Usually, we're not too troubled by the question of assurance when everything is going well. We feel that we're deserving, and everything's the way it should be. However, for many of us, this all changes as we go through the "valley of the shadow of death" for long periods of time. Our conscience becomes more sensitized and begins to scream out against us that we're not faithful enough, loving enough, believing enough, or whatever other deficiency it might think of. It's during these periods that we see our ugliness in 3-D and conclude that we're totally unworthy of God. We feel condemned by our moral failures and convinced that God too condemns us.

This had been the very problem of a young, sixteenth century Augustinian monk. This young man had just completed law school and from all indications had a brilliant career awaiting him. However, one evening while walking between villages, he was struck down by a bolt of lightening and feared for his eternal destiny. In those days, the surest way to ensure that you were going to make it to heaven was to give up everything that you owned and to become a monk. This is just what the young man did. However, his experience didn't match his expectations. He had expected that having made such a sacrificial move, he would have found himself transformed and assured of salvation. However, he found himself unchanged, struggling with the same inner darkness and temptations that had always been his companions. He strenuously devoted himself to the spiritual disciplines of fasting, prayer, and to other forms of self-denial, all to no avail. He later commented that on several occasions he had driven himself to the point of death.

Subsequently, the youth spent hours in confession daily. The vicar, Johann Von Staupitz, would lovingly advise him to not worry about all his little sins, but to just return to confession only when he had some big sins to confess. However, the monk, aware of the perfect righteousness of God, knew that he was far from attaining it. He therefore resorted to confession on a daily basis. Finally, Von Staupitz reasoned, "All you have to do is just love God."

To this the young monk responded, "Love Him? I hate Him!" Luther believed that no matter how hard he tried to please God, God would never accept him.

Von Staupitz concluded that the gifted Luther would be best off if he could serve others and began to guide him on the road that would eventually lead Luther to become a professor at the newly commissioned Wittenberg University. Once there, Luther commenced upon a pivotal study of the Book of Romans. In this study, he came upon a verse that would change his life: "The righteous shall live by faith."[1] He saw that it was not a matter of attaining the unattainable, but accepting as a free gift what had previously seemed unacceptable. He later wrote that it was as if he had passed through the doors of heaven itself. His life was changed and with it the history of Europe and Christianity. He had rediscovered a simple truth that had seemed too good to be true: our Maker had paid the price in full. In a burst, Luther came to realize that it wasn't about our deeds or worthiness, but about a God who had bought our love and devotion through His own.

Feelings of unworthiness, shame, and rejection have driven many to despair, even suicide. There were many occasions when I prowled the dark of the night, away from the scrutiny of others, seeking solace. This was partially because I didn't regard these feelings as alien intruders but as learned professors who were preaching truth. For a while, they convinced me that God must be a sadist. There was no other explanation for my pain.

My problem was twofold. I hadn't yet sufficiently understood and believed what my true Professor was teaching me about Himself and His salvation. The second problem was that I wasn't convinced that these teachings applied to me. Perhaps God had found something utterly distasteful about me that precluded salvation; or perhaps I hadn't believed or repented with the depth or purity that were required. The former was an objective problem, the latter, a subjective one. Let me first address the objective problem briefly.

Scripture portrays a God who is truly disposed to love and forgive us. The best testimony to this fact is the Cross. God came, was rejected, and died for His enemies. Paul reasons that if He died for us and paid the supreme price for us while we rejected and crucified Him, how much more, now that the price has been paid and our hearts have been disposed to value Him, is He desirous of us.[2] He is so desirous that *"all* who call upon the Name of the Lord shall be saved."[3] If you buy a junk car and invest years and your savings into restoring it to its original, aren't you going to value it far more now than when it was lying in the junk heap along with countless other hunks of metal? Aren't you now going to be far more protective of what has become your pride and joy? We too have been regenerated from enemies and liabilities into objects of love and delight.

Jesus says that any who come to Him, he receives. Any junk heap that cries out to be rescued will be accepted. The logic is simple. The precious price paid by Christ with His own life is infinite, enough to purchase all the junk heaps in existence. Why then wouldn't He want to maximize His purchase by receiving all the junk heaps that come to Him?"[4]

This is in answer to the objective question about the offer of salvation. However, my focus in this chapter is the second question, the subjective one: "How do I how that I've 'come' to Him or that I've believed as I should?" This question is fueled by verses that indicate that it's possible to make a confession of faith without truly believing:

> "Not everyone who says to Me, 'Lord, Lord,' shall enter the kingdom of heaven, but he who does the will of My Father in heaven. Many will say to Me in that day, 'Lord, Lord, have we not prophesied in Your name, cast out demons in Your name, and done many wonders in Your name?' And then I will declare to them, 'I never knew you; depart from Me, you who practice lawlessness!'"[5]

In light of this troubling warning (and others like it), how can I know I'm truly saved despite the myriad objective assurances that if I believe, I'm saved? The Bible tells me if I "come," or "believe," or "repent," or "confess" I shall be saved. But haven't the others who proclaimed "Lord, Lord" also done these things? How do I know that my faith is real enough, or my repentance is deep enough, or my coming is sincere enough? Yes, sometimes I feel that God is with me. But sometimes I also feel that He isn't and I feel condemned."

It's normal to experience doubt and condemnation even as a child of God. John warns us that our conscience may erroneously condemn us even when we've been entirely forgiven by God. "For if our heart condemns us, God is greater than our heart, and knows all things."[6] John understood that our conscience isn't a perfect guide. It might have been badly skewed by our life experiences. Ultimately, God is the One who counts, not our conscience. He's the final arbiter. His Word goes!

In such cases we must correct our conscience by preaching a God-informed sermon to it. David, in the throes of despair, often did this very thing:

"Why are you cast down, O my soul? And why are you disquieted within me? Hope in God; for I shall yet praise Him, the help of my countenance and my God."[7]

David well knew that the "soul" can become hysterical for no good cause. It required so reassurance and loving reminders.

What should this sermon include? All the assurances of Scripture! We must inform our conscience that people don't come to God, period! Unless God has drawn us, we can't come.[8] "I've come, so I must belong to God! If I didn't belong to God, I wouldn't care less about my relationship with Him. The fact that I care proves that God has done a work in my life.[9] Scripture asserts that people love the untruths of darkness more than truth itself.[10] "I read the Bible. I want to know God's truth, even when it says things that don't flatter me. This isn't the natural way people respond to the Bible. Those who don't love truth run from God. Therefore, I must belong to Him."

Loraine Boettner advised those who doubt to ask themselves this question: "What is my attitude toward Christ? Would I be glad for Him to appear and talk personally to me this moment? Would I welcome Him as my friend, or would I shrink from meeting Him? Those who look forward with joy to the coming of Christ may know that they are saved."[11]

Of course, with all the demonic assistance readily available, our conscience will be preaching it's own sermon: "Look at you! Your faith is a sham! You would be ashamed to have Christ come to you. You have more doubt there than anything else. You don't really love God; you're just in it for what you can get out of it! What type of love is that?"

The Devil preaches a powerful sermon, one full of condemnation. In order to respond adequately, we need to be clothed in the truths of the Word of God. (And the more we're attacked, the more we'll become so clad!)

So often, I had found myself torn to shreds, wanting to die. Now, I merely respond, "Devil, you're perfectly correct. My faith is inadequate and my motives are largely self-serving, but Jesus has died for me for this very reason. My righteousness is totally inadequate, but His is more than enough. You can condemn me all you want, but this only makes me adore my Savior all the more! You merely remind me of what I've left behind and to the Grace that now surrounds me!"

The Devil will press on, "How can you know you're saved? One is saved by faith, but you don't have enough faith. You're just playing "make-believe" because it makes you feel good. You're selfish and your faith is about you, not about God or even about anyone else!"

I respond, "Yes, I've come to God for purely selfish reasons. I'm as a little babe who requires every manner of nurturing. But it's my Father's delight to provide this very thing. He loves me that, in due time, I might return that love to Him, and by doing so love others."

How much faith do we need? Jesus said that if we have the faith the size of a mustard seed, we can move mountains and mulberry trees.[12] The mustard seed was the smallest seed around. Jesus was saying that the smallest amount imaginable was enough. This principle is exemplified by what we find in the "hall of fame of faith." We find Sarah, who, "By faith...received strength to conceive seed, and bore a child when she was past the age, because she judged Him faithful who had promised."[13]

But there's something the matter with this picture! When we read the original account, Sarah disbelieved, laughed to herself, and then lied to God, saying she hadn't laughed when she had heard the divine promises— not quite a convincing portrait of faith. Yet, Sarah is commemorated for her faith.[14]

We also find Isaac proudly displayed in the "hall of fame": "By faith Isaac blessed Jacob and Esau concerning things to come."[15] Indeed, to have proclaimed the destiny of his two sons would have required an exercise of faith. However, again something is the matter with this picture. When we read the Genesis account of this event, we see very little evidence of faith. What we do see is Isaac stubbornly intending to give the blessing of God to Esau, because he preferred Esau and his cooking, rather than to Jacob. (A good case can be made for the fact that Isaac should have known that the blessing belonged to Jacob, but Isaac wanted to stubbornly pursue his own agenda!) However, in his physical and spiritual blindness, he was deceived into giving the blessing to Jacob. It wasn't until Esau appeared on the scene expecting the blessing that his eyes were "opened" and Isaac realized what had happened. It was only then that he realized that what he had done was irreversible. He had providentially blessed *God's* own choice and recognized this as the will of God.

How is it then that they appear in this "hall of fame" if their faith is so questionable? How can they serve as an example for the rest of us? It is our saving, loving, and dying God who is the *example*. It is our God who condescends to stoop down and to love those who are utterly unworthy of Him and bestows upon them significance and honor for the most shabby contributions imaginable. "Yes, Devil, my faith is quite laughable, but this laughable faith is in my Redeemer, who is well pleased with it."

The "hall of fame" then goes on to showcase Moses who "by faith forsook Egypt, not fearing the wrath of the king, for he endured as seeing Him who is invisible."[16] However, when we read this account in the book of Exodus, we read, "And He feared...Moses fled from the face of Pharaoh."[17] Again, how do we reconcile these uniformly consistent but divergent perspectives? Why do these "fathers" of the faith look so different from a New Testament perspective? It's because we get a clearer understanding of the compassion of God in those pages. It is God who has mercy on us stumbling human creations and graciously finds within us something pleasing!

The next subjects to be paraded forth from the "hall of Fame" are the children of Israel who "by faith...passed through the Red Sea as by dry land..."[18] At the risk of sounding monotonous, let me refer back to the Exodus account where we find that at the brink of the Red Sea with the Egyptians in pursuit, the Israelites accused Moses of bringing them out into the wilderness to die. They also reminded him that they hadn't wanted to leave, but that it was all Moses' idea that they leave the relative comforts of Egypt.[19] Nevertheless, they passed through the sea. Their faith wasn't commendable in any objective sense, but it was a faith in God. God had placed them between a rock and a split sea. As much as they had wanted to return to Egypt, salvation now demanded that they pass through the sea. They lacked the faith in themselves to confront the Egyptians or to trust in any other plan that they might hatch at this point. As much as they hated to do it, their eyes had to be placed in trust upon God to get them across to safety on the other side. It wasn't so much the amount of their faith or even the soundness of it but that theirs was a faith in God.

Our faith is never perfect, but God is. Our attitudes continue to affront God, but He is infinitely patient. "Yes, Devil, there is nothing in me worthy of God except for the fact that God is with me and will continue His work of love,[20] making up for all my deficiencies. I stand in the righteousness of God alone in Whom there is no condemnation."[21]

It's not a matter of the quantity of faith, but a matter of direction. Everyone has faith in something. If our hope is in God rather than in ourselves, job, or money, we can preach to ourselves, "I am in Him and He is in me!" and "Thanks be to God that He's closed the familiar door of self-trust that I might be coerced to resort to the only true Trust!"

How then are we to understand the exclusion of those crying, "Lord, Lord?" Jesus' miracles could have filled His bandwagon many times over, but for all the wrong reasons. He had miraculously produced bread and fish for all on at least two occasions. As a result the hordes followed Him, but He lamented, "Most assuredly I say to you, you seek Me not because you saw the signs, but because you ate the loaves and were filled."[22] They had no stomach for Jesus and His gift of forgiveness, but only for His bread. He didn't want to be followed for merely carnal reasons, so He began to preach that they had to eat His flesh and to drink His blood. These difficult sayings achieved their intended purpose and drove the masses away.

Sometimes people tagged along solely for the power they hoped to receive. The Book of Acts describes the seven sons of Sceva who were in it for the power to cast out demons.[23] Simon the magician was also in it for the power of the miraculous gifts.[24] First century Christianity was a "tour de force," an unstoppable bandwagon with fireworks and excitement, and everybody was jumping on. The Roman Empire eventually made the jump. Those who had addressed Jesus as "Lord, Lord," He called "workers of iniquity." They were planning evil even as they gave lip service to Jesus. They had no stomach for His Gospel. "Yes, Devil, I am no more worthy than these, but God has given me desire to be morally clean and to be with the Light eternally. This doesn't make me any more deserving than others. It just makes me blessed beyond words."

We can reassure ourselves on the basis of our faith. The book of First John was written to assure the followers that they have eternal life.

- "By this you know the Spirit of God: Every spirit that confesses that Jesus Christ has come in the flesh is of God."[25]

- "Whoever confesses that Jesus is the Son of God, God abides in him, and he in God."[26]

- "He who believes in the Son of God has the witness in himself; he who does not believe God has made Him a liar, because he has not believed the testimony that God has given of His Son. And this is the testimony: that God has given us eternal life, and this life is in His Son."[27]

Faith is not only the means of receiving the free gift; it also serves to assure us that we have it. We also find assurance in the lives we lead.

"Now by this we know that we *know* Him, if we keep His commandments. He who says, 'I know Him,' but doesn't keep His commandments, is a liar, and the truth is not in him. But whoever keeps His word, truly the love of God is perfected in him. By this we *know* that we are in Him. He who says he abides in Him ought himself also to walk just as He walked."[28]

We're not saved by our obedience but reassured by it. This is because where there is faith, there will also follow obedience to that faith. Where obedience is lacking, our assurance will also be lacking to some degree. In order to secure a deeper sense of assurance that we're in God, Peter advises us to confirm our salvation through the way we live our lives.[29]

Walking in love is so important that I think that God has designed things in such a way that we won't experience full joy and assurance of His love until we begin to live our lives as Jesus did. The more we walk in love, the more we'll feel in unity with Jesus, and the less we'll fear death and judgment. John writes,

> "Love has been perfected among us in this: that we may have boldness in the day of judgment, because as He is, so are we in this world."[30]

We find great encouragement and assurance when we see Christ's life embodied in our own behavior. It shouldn't be otherwise. God has designed our lives in such a way that we gain deeper levels of assurance and joy as we devote our lives to the love He's called us to.

> "For God is not unjust so as to forget your work and the love which you have shown toward His name, in having ministered and in still ministering to the saints. And we desire that each one of you show the same diligence so as *to realize the full assurance* of hope until the end."[31]
> (Italics mine)

This suggests that insofar as we fail to devote ourselves in love, we will also deprive ourselves of the assurance of God's love. There are great joys in living like Jesus did. Jesus stated that He derived joy from serving His Father.[32] (This doesn't rule out the fact that there is also suffering.)

Deacons were assured that through their service, they would be amply rewarded. "For those who have served well as deacons obtain for themselves a good standing and *great boldness* in the faith which is in Christ Jesus."[33] (Italics mine) This is true for any faithfulness.

Assurance is something we may have to grow into. Lack of it serves as a painful prod, a goad against complacency. Diligence requires some degree of discomfort. Without discomfort, we tend to remain in our own dirty clothes. It's improbable that Luther would have played the pivotal role to which he had been called without the goad of his personal turmoil. "Salvation by grace through faith alone" would never have become his burning issue had it not been for his painful doubts regarding his own salvation. Forgiveness would never seemed so utterly beautiful had Luther never wrestled with his own unworthiness before a perfect God.

It's been a long and slow haul for me. I had often despaired because it was so slow and because I could see no purpose for it, nor any good coming out of it. Only in retrospect can I begin to see what He has accomplished through it. David had said, "It is good that I have been afflicted that I might learn your statutes."[34]

SOME PROBLEMS:

1. *"I can't stop worrying and obsessing about myself. It's just in my nature that I can't find peace with God."*

God is greater than our nature, problems, or the effects of our upbringing. Yes, some of us are more fearful than others, but God is able to turn any minus into a plus. He allowed you to have your worrying, obsessing nature for a reason and if it suits His loving plan for your life, He can remove it in an instance. Meanwhile, God will use these burdens to mold you into the person He wants you to be.

For the meantime, look towards Him and His promises to you: "...Neither death nor life, nor angels nor principalities nor powers, nor things present nor things to come, nor height nor depth, nor any created thing shall be able to separate us from the love of God which is in Christ Jesus our Lord."[35]

2. *"I'm so screwed up and absorbed with my own needs and pains that I can't walk in love."*

God is able to make you walk.[36] There's nothing He can't do. If God can raise up new believers from stones, our limitations and weaknesses are nothing for Him. Just keep waiting for God's deliverance.[37]

Everything good that we have comes from the grace of God. Paul stated that he is what he is purely because of what God did in him,[38] and he was no more deserving than any of us.[39]

3. *"I've failed so many times that I think He's washed His hands of me."*

The price has already been paid for our sins. It costs God nothing additionally to forgive your sins. In fact, He glories in showing His favor to those crushed by their own sense of unworthiness. He's close to the broken-hearted.

Avail yourself of His ever-present promise: "If we confess our sins, He is faithful and just to forgive us our sins and to cleanse us from all unrighteousness."[40]

EXERCISE

1. In what ways have you struggled with doubts about your relationship with God?

2. Have you seen any good coming out of this struggle? What good could possibly be accomplished through it?

3. What other issues must yet be resolved for you to have some sense of peace?

[1] Romans 1:17

[2] Rom. 5:8-10

[3] Rom. 10:13

[4] John 6:37-40

[5] Matthew 7:21-23

[6] 1 John 3:20

[7] Psalm 42:11

[8] John 6:44

[9] 1 Cor. 2:14

[10] John 3:19-21

[11] The Reformed Doctrine of Predestination, Loraine Boettner, Presbyterian and Reformed Publishing Co., Phillipsburg, NJ

[12] Luke 17:6

[13] Heb. 11:11

[14] Gen. 18:15

[15] Gen. 11:20

[16] Heb. 11:27

[17] Exodus 2:14-15

[18] Heb. 11:29

[19] Exodus 14:11-12

[20] Phil. 1:6

[21] Rom. 8:1

[22] John 6:26

[23] Acts 19:14

[24] Acts 8:19

[25] 1 John 4:2

[26] 1 John 4:15

[27] 1 John 5:10-11

[28] 1 John 2:3-6

[29] 2 Pet. 1:10

[30] 1 John 4:17

[31] Heb. 6:10-11

[32] John 4:34

[33] 1 Tim. 3:13

[34] Psalm 119:71

[35] Rom. 8:38-39
[36] Rom. 14:4
[37] Psalm 46:10
[38] 1 Cor. 15:10
[39] 1 Tim. 1:15
[40] 1 John 1:9

CHAPTER 12

Reassurance Along the Path

> "Good and upright is the Lord. Therefore He teaches sinners in the way. The humble He guides in justice, and the humble He teaches His way." **Psalm 25:8-9**

Recently, Anita and I went hiking in the Adirondacks. At times, it became difficult to discern the path. We couldn't be sure that we were on a path at all. However, my agitation was soothed when we came to the characteristic path marker on a tree. I felt reassured. Life was again 'good'. Anita can tolerate a lot more uncertainty than I, but at times, she too needs to know we're going in the right direction.

The Christian life is no different. No, it's worse. We're instructed what markers to look for, but we don't find them. Paul tells us, "The Spirit Himself bears witness with our spirit that we are children of God,"[1] but for the most part, we don't feel it. Peter tells us, "You rejoice with joy inexpressible and full of glory,"[2] but we seldom see this either. Have we gotten off the path?

We all need reassurance that we're still on the path, when we can't seem to find the markers. What does this reassurance consist of when we don't experience peace and everything is confusion? Without the regularly spaced tree markers, we had to find less obvious indications that we were on the right path. We assumed that the real path was more well worn than the deer trials and rabbit holes. In most cases, we were correct.

The Christian life is similar. Sometimes we have to find reassurance in secondary markers. Let me propose one such set of markers or blueprint that might make sense out of the darkness.

QUADRANT #1 Law	#2 Obedience
#4 Grace	#3 Repentance

This is a blueprint of the Christian life. If we measure our life against it, it might serve to calm our souls and to direct our anxious steps. We start out in quadrant #1 where we're presented with a list of our responsibilities. We learn that we have to forgive others and make reparations for the things we've done wrong. This brings us to the application, quadrant #2. With zeal we plunge forward and find that doing the law is sweet. We find that as we walk in obedience our relationships improve. We're thrilled to find that we can exercise some meaningful control over our lives. We return to square #1 to learn more about what's expected of us. We learn that we're supposed to give unselfishly and to love even our enemies. Taking these new insights into quadrant #2, we begin to apply them to our lives and find that even some of our enemies are beginning to soften in their attitudes about us. Victory! Back to # 1 for some more instruction about our responsibilities! We're energized! We're sure that this Christian life is the best thing we've ever found. We're feeling spiritual and confident that God is very pleased with us.

Sooner or later, we begin to hit our heads against a brick wall. We try to be obedient, but it's just not working out the way it used to. We decide that we'll have to dig in a bit more and to try a little harder, but again we reach an impasse, and frustration and despair set in. We don't feel quite as spiritual as we did before. We're not quite as excited about God as we had been, and we're sure that He's not quite as excited about us. We begin to see that even where our outward performance looks good, our motives are self-serving. We're more concerned about how we look than how others feel. When we read Jesus' denunciations of the Pharisees, we know that this pertains also to us, but we try to justify ourselves. We try to prove to ourselves that we're different and somehow more deserving than the Pharisees. Indeed, we must be if we're going to inherit the kingdom of God.[3]

Those who are more excited about God than we tend to irritate us. Rather than rejoicing in their spiritual triumphs, we find that we're jealous, but we reassure ourselves that there are justifiable reasons for our jealousy.

I became very disturbed by others who I felt were talking over-confidently about their faith and performance. They were making everything that was frustrating me sound so facile. Lacking in love, I set ambushes for them by asking them questions that would lead them into contradiction. Then I'd pounce. One friend still remembers such an encounter 25 years earlier. Thankfully, we can now laugh about it together.

As the frustration and disappointment mounts, we try to find other coping mechanisms. If we don't, the frustration may be followed by despair and depression. We can satisfy ourselves with the reassurance that although we're not perfect, most others are far worse. Although this devise works in the short run, in the long run it's psychological suicide. If our value as a person depends upon how we measure up against others, we've condemned ourselves to obsessively look both to ourselves and others in a vain attempt to assure ourselves that we are maintaining our superiority. We've banished ourselves from the mercy of God to the whims of a lesser god, ourselves. If we come out smelling like a rose, we become supercilious and self-righteous. If we come out smelling like a sewer, we despair. Neither result is desirable.

Another popular response is to change the law, which condemns our failures, or at least to reinterpret it. The Pharisees, according to Jesus, were experts on promoting the parts of the Law that made them look good, conveniently obscuring the more demanding aspects of the Law.[4] They were adept at performing righteously in the public to receive public acclaim. This served to reinforce their distorted, self-righteous self-adulation.[5]

We too tend to slide into our own forms of self-righteousness. Arguing that Jesus doesn't want us to feel guilty and insecure, we reinterpret New Testament teachings so that they feel more comfortable to us. We no longer have to be like Jesus, because when we try to be like Jesus, we fail and then feel guilty. Certainly, Jesus doesn't want that!

We don't have to love everyone because that's impractical. In this way, we reformulate the law so that we can feel good about our performance even though it stinks.

If we succeed, we can stay in the first two quadrants without sinking into the more radical, unbelievable, and messy aspects of the bottom two quadrants. This type of "success" will allow us to live with our self-righteousness and avoid a painful reexamination.

There is nothing the matter with the first two quadrants. They're biblical! The Law is beautiful, holy, and able to convert the soul,[6] and those who love God will keep His Word.[7] *Remaining* in these two quadrants is the problem.

It was never intended that we would achieve righteousness through following the law. Neither are we able to legitimately obtain our sense of significance from it. The law came to show us our brokenness and our inability to please God without trusting in His mercy.[8] By showing us our need for a Savior, the law would lead us to faith in Christ. How would the law do this? For one thing, it would provoke even more sin in us, thereby showing us our helplessness.[9]

It's sinful to remain in the first two quadrants; it's a refusal to see our sin, to see our delusions, arrogance, and self-righteousness. It's a willingness to live a truncated existence where lies reign supreme and relationships become just as superficial as we've become. It represents a rejection of everything God is trying to show us and wants to give us.

Jesus told a story about two men who entered the temple. One was a religious leader. He was self-righteous, trusting in his own accomplishments and looking down upon others. Jesus said that this man "prayed with himself,"[10] engaging in some form of auto-stimulation. Although he thought he was praying to God, he was merely practicing a ritual to reinforce his own delusions of superiority. In his prayer, he reminded himself of the fact that he was superior to a whole list of people including the traitor of a tax collector who was appropriately humbling himself in the other corner.

In contrast, the tax collector knew he was a broken, needy man. He didn't appeal to any merit on his part. He knew he had none. He could only cry out for God's undeserved mercy.

Of the two, Jesus declared that it was only the tax collector who left the temple forgiven. Why? Was the tax collector any more deserving than the religious leader? Certainly not, but the tax collector had despaired of the first two quadrants and of his own ability to perform. He also had the advantage that society was telling him that he was a "loser." In his situation, it was more difficult to convince himself otherwise. He despaired of being able to claim any merit before God. He had fallen through the floor into quadrant #3. He now had to believe in a God more merciful than he had any right to imagine. He had to repent of his entire life and to admit that he was entirely unworthy. He had to come to a demanding God without any meritorious offering. He had to come in his stinking clothes to an elite gathering without any gift to guarantee his welcome. He knew he wasn't deserving. What hope could he possibly have of a joyous welcome?

No one wants to go there. It's just too painful. Any lie is preferable to seeing that we're naked and destitute. But when the lie eludes, we're left clinging to an unbelievable hope that there might be a God who will have mercy. We know we're undeserving and that we shouldn't expect anything, but it doesn't cost anything to ask. That's the only option left to us.

For years, I clung pathetically to a hope that I might deserve something for my good works. I was working with teenagers through a Big Brother program. I had certainly heard about grace and even marginally believed in it, but not enough to risk foregoing any of my "religious" duties. I felt that I was barely holding on by a thread and didn't have the credit with God to ease up for a moment. If I did, there was no telling what would happen to me. I certainly thought about grace, but it was just too risky. It was safer to rely upon my efforts. God would certainly respect them and the pain I was enduring for His sake. I would hedge my bets. Marginally, I'd believed in grace, but just to "play it safe" I'd also accrue my own merit.

Graciously, God had kept the youth from seeing my deepest motivations, which were more driven by fear than by anything else. This isn't the type of faith we're supposed to have. Paul criticized the Galatian church for mixing and matching. They had started with a pure faith in Christ but then began to entertain ideas of meriting God's blessings. They were committing the cardinal sin: denying that what Christ had accomplished was a *complete* gift of righteousness, forgiveness, and reconciliation with God. Paul so was horrified by this turnabout that he cried, "Have you suffered so many things in vain!"[11]

The law and our filthy rags of obedience must lead us repentantly to quadrant #3 if our eyes are open. I had to first convince myself that I wouldn't be struck dead by lightening if I took a rest from my "good deed." For me, the process was gradual. The more I unburdened myself of these deeds (I had begun to see that they were worthless as a source of merit), the more I was forced to trust alone in this unseen God. It was unsettling for a long time, but He gradually led me into quadrant #4 where I began to see the Gospel in a new light. I began to see that I was failing to hedge my bets. Safety abode in trusting God alone by forsaking any claim I might have had to His mercy.

Abraham had merely taken the words of God at face value and he was declared righteous apart from anything he had done to deserve this.[12] David was reconciled back to God despite the heinousness of his sins by merely trusting in Him.[13] Certainly the grievousness of David's sins had exhausted any merit he might have earned, but he was forgiven. Perhaps there was a chance for me? It was hard to take such a dive into the darkness. Trusting in my own merit seemed to be the surer path; at least it had looked this way before. I was beginning to see myself in a progressively worse light. Consequently, it became harder to believe in my own merit.

Comparing notes with others, I saw this as the very work of God— to humble us that He might exalt us. Humility must precede honor or honor becomes contaminated by the baggage we import into our Christian lives. Had God blessed me with His peace while I was still trusting in my own righteous contributions, He would have enabled me to believe that it was *I myself* who had triumphed.

As I began to look into quadrant #4, I increasingly found things of great and startling beauty. I saw portraits of forgiveness that I hadn't thought possible. I saw King Manasseh, arguably the most bloodthirsty of Judah's kings, forgiven by God and restored. The Assyrians had thrown him into prison. There, in his pain, he humbled himself and cried out to God who forgave him and restored to him his throne.[14] If anybody had been an enemy of God, it was Manasseh. For years he had God's own prophets murdered. It is said that he even had Isaiah sawn in two.

I also came to be awe-struck by the omnipotence of God. He had everything under control. I didn't have to worry about a thing, even about my own failings. He was able to work *everything* together for my good. Jesus assured His own fearful disciples that their worry was completely needless. Not even a sparrow could fall to the ground without God's OK. If God cared so much about sparrows, wouldn't it follow that He cared about us so much more?[15]

Finding encouragement in God's grace doesn't stop there. We're now ready to return to quadrant #1 and again to survey the divine commands. But this time it's different. We begin to see that our good works aren't so much our gift to God, but His gift to us! We find that it's a joy and a privilege to serve God. Jesus even said that He derived nourishment from this.[16] Also, we approach our obedience to the law with a new motivation. We've learned that we can't earn anything from God, but something else begins to take its place. We begin to find a deeper sense of gratitude for His grace, a gratitude that can only grow out of the knowledge of our hopeless condition.

Henry Herzog, a Holocaust survivor, wrote from his new-found home in the United States, "I am alive today due to the courage of three Gentile Poles." When he returned to his former home in Rzeszow he paid his respects to two of his rescuers by prostrating himself upon their graves.[17] The more we understand our hopelessness and our salvation by the sheer grace of God, the more the gratitude leads us to prostrate our lives before Him.

With this lesson under our belt, we're now confident that things will begin to go more smoothly. But again we're brought to our knees! We're not doing as well as we had thought that we would. We begin to see that our heart is quite divided. What we thought we had been doing out of love, we find that we were really pursuing the praise of people. Again, we find ourselves crushed and fall through the floor to quadrant #3 where, all over again, we repent of our sins. This continues to happen and we begin to wonder if God can really use such a filthy vessel as we have now found ourselves to be.

He opens our eyes up once again in quadrant #4. We begin to see that God will never give up on us. We look at Jacob's life to find that after many years of conniving, he emerges from his cocoon of deceit a humble man of faith.

Now we feel encouraged again to climb back into quadrant #1 to see what else God wants us to do. Eventually, discouraged again, we're back on our knees in quadrant #3 wondering whether there's any hope for us, total failures that we are. We find that there is hope and the cycle repeats itself again. Nevertheless, we're coming to repentance quicker each time. The treadmill is frustrating, but we begin to see that it's necessary for our spiritual health. Praising God becomes easier and more heart-felt as we see Him as our only hope.

Notice that each quadrant is necessary. The law and our failed obedience to it allow grace to truly be grace. Just try forgiving someone who doesn't think he's done anything wrong. He'll just take the forgiveness as an accusation of wrongdoing. We will not see God's grace as what it truly is unless we see our real predicament. Quadrant #4 wouldn't have come alive to me without the brokenness of quadrant #3. I couldn't have come to #3 without the frustration of trying to be a good Christian (#2). I could never have come to this frustration and disappointment without the commands of quadrant #1. Furthermore, I would have rejected the commandments along with my Christian life if it hadn't been for the grace of #4.

We may not always feel the love, joy, and peace that are part of our inheritance, but the full understanding of God's workings is a vital roadmap to reassure us along our sometimes-painful journey.

I've been writing about how the light of the understanding of God's ways helps us penetrate the fog to illuminate and comfort. However, there are times when darkness surrounds to the point of suffocation, when the light of understanding entirely fails, and when our emotions become savage assailants. At such times, all we can do is let faith soar to its natural resting place unimpeded by our grasping and frustrated understanding. There have been times when the only thing I could do was to crawl into my bed with the Bible and to read the fleeting words until I was granted some spark of hope.

SOME COMMON PROBLEMS ENCOUNTERED ON THE PATH:

1. *"I'm a complete failure. I just don't have what it takes to follow God."*

   - Although it doesn't feel good, this is actually a wonderful understanding to have (John 15:4-5).
   - God delights in taking our weaknesses and failures and turning them around completely (2 Cor. 12:9-10). What seems so monumental to us is nothing in His hands.
   - God takes the most broken of people and establishes them (Rom 14:4; Dan. 4:32). The lives of the Patriarchs are good examples of this.

2. *"I just don't seem to be spiritual enough to follow God's lead or to hear His voice."*

- You don't have to hear His voice. God is able to perfectly lead you and perfect even without your knowledge. He uses people who don't even believe He exists to accomplish His plans. Just look at Pharaoh. God is able to bring locusts and fowls where He wants them to be. Can't He do that with us?
- He promises to lead and restore us (Psalm 23). Therefore, it's not about us; it's about God. Just marvel at His greatness and His beauty through His Word.

3. *"I've failed so many times, I just can't get the hope together to even read the Bible or to pray."*

- Sometimes, all we can do is to wait for God to rescue us (Psalm 46:10). Accept your weakness and failures. It's all part of the plan. God rejoices in lifting us up after we completely despair of self (1 Cor. 1:26-30).
- Meanwhile, as best as you can, look at portraits of how God has rescued others who were utterly powerless. In many cases they had already given up hope. Even though Jesus had warned them that they would turn away (Mat. 26:31), when the events did take place, they nevertheless lost hope that Jesus would ever return to them. Even when we lose hope, it doesn't mean that there's no hope. God is faithful!

4. *"There are many things in Scripture that are confusing to me. These tend to undermine any sense of faith that I might have."*

- This is understandable. That's why we need to be established in the truths of the faith (Eph. 4:11-14). Although not every area of uncertainty will be resolved in this life, in due time you'll find that you'll have the

understanding you require.
- Meanwhile, know that the confusion that you're experiencing serves to provoke your further investigations.

EXERCISE:

1. Have you come to an understanding that God's ways are perfect? Do the four quadrants help or hinder in this?

2. Does it help to understand God's ways? What does it feel like when your experience doesn't make any Biblical sense?

3. Does a Biblical understanding encourage your faith? How?

4. What truths about God have been the greatest encouragements to your faith?

---

[1] Rom. 8:16
[2] 1 Peter 1:8
[3] Mat. 5:20
[4] Mat. 23:23
[5] Mat. 6:1-4
[6] Psalm 119; Rom. 7:12
[7] John 14:21-24
[8] Rom. 3:19-20
[9] Gal. 3:21-24
[10] Luke 18:11
[11] Gal. 3:4. Obedience is an important part of the Christian life. However, we must do good deeds for the right reasons. It must never be a substitute for trusting God.
[12] Rom. 4:2-5
[13] Rom. 4:6-8
[14] 2 Chron. 33:13
[15] Mat. 10:29-30

[16] John 4:34

[17] <u>The Righteous, The Unsung Heroes of the Holocaust</u>, Martin Gilbert, Henry Holt and Company, NY, NY, 2003, pg. 127.

Part 2:

CHRISTIANITY

AND

SECULAR THERAPY

CHAPTER 13

Therapy and Reversing Repression

> "Fixing our eyes on Jesus, the author and perfecter of faith, who for the joy set before Him endured the cross, despising the shame, and has sat down at the right hand of the throne of God." **Hebrews 12:2**

Seeking truth should be high on the Christian priority list, whether from the divine book of Scripture or from the divine book of life or creation. But how do we find truth? Does it come by bringing to light repressed material or by achieving some cathartic release?

If I was going to have such an experience it should have been through Orgone Therapy. Wilhelm Reich was a disciple of Sigmund Freud. I've been told that he had been Freud's ablest student. Eventually, he broke away from Freud and developed something he called "Orgone Therapy." Orgonomy is based on the understanding that we're encapsulated by successive layers of socialization, which have to be stripped away in order to uncover the real person. Reich believed that neuroses were maintained by means of muscular blockages. These could be unblocked through emotionally engaging our past, by having some form of cathartic experience, screaming, crying, or clawing our way through the blockage.

How was the cathartic experience brought about? There was

very little talking. I would undress to the point of my underwear. (I would have gone farther if the cure had depended upon it!) I was then instructed to hyperventilate. Emotions were supposed to arise through this process and all I had to do was to let them come and stay with them as a surfer on his wave. The more emotion that I could discharge through the process, the better.

The methodology was simple. The therapist sat behind me, painfully squeezing my shoulder muscles as if he was trying to squeeze dried glue from a tube. The poison glue could then be sloughed aside through a burst of emotion. His painful manipulations were supposed to prime me to release some angry feelings, and not surprisingly, he occasionally succeeded. Yet, after each session, I descended back into the same humdrum existence.

One day I arrived for therapy and asked the therapist a question: "Was there anything I could do to hasten along the therapy?" Without missing a beat, he answered, "Just sit back and leave the driving to me." I allowed him to do the driving for the next half-year, but we merely seemed to be spinning our wheels. I must admit that I did have one experience that I thought was cathartic. In the course of hyperventilating, I began to cry uncontrollably through the balance of the session. When I had finished, it felt as if the clouds had all parted and I could see the sun for the first time. I left cheered and hopeful that this was a new beginning, but the new beginning lasted for just a couple of hours. I was left with no net gain, as far as I could tell.

For the next several years, I faithfully continued the practices that I had learned during my previous years in secular therapy. I strenuously analyzed my dreams and anything else that I could dredge up.

There are several dangers involved in the hunt for repressed memories and other thoughts. For one thing, what we unearth might not be memories at all but imaginations. This is now often alleged where therapists, believing sexual abuse to be the root cause of a problem, coached their clients into producing "memories."

Elizabeth Loftus believes that many abuse narratives are actually concoctions. She was able to demonstrate that "memories" could often be experimentally induced. She "posits that the rising of repressed memories is really a concatenation of fantasy, fear, innuendo, and news with wisps of truth woven in."[1]

Even our un-coaxed memories have been shown to be very unreliable. We all have selective filters that tend to skew the events one way or another. We're selective about what we remember and selective about how we remember it. We're also reductionistic. We prefer simple explanations and like to remake the past into the paradigms the already support our assessments of the past. This gives us the much sought after sense that things fit together. It might be that our newly discovered memories are no memories at all.

But they often feel like memories, and they seem to have a therapeutic effect! This might be that we have such a powerful need to find an explanation and an answer to our pain and dysfunction.

> "We concoct stories at all costs, because we need to, because we have to. So powerful is the need to have a socially sanctioned narrative that we will adopt one even if it means we are the villain at its center."[2]

Hunting for truth in the wrong places is risky business. It reminds me of my brief experience with the Ouji Board. I was 22 years old and light years away from a belief in Christ. I had an on-and-off-again girlfriend who could work the Ouji with anyone. We were fascinated by the speed with which our spirit contacts could spell our answers. Their vulgarity didn't put us off. In our naiveté, we just assumed that such transcendent beings had a sense of humor that we weren't evolved enough to grasp.

My parent's home had just been burglarized so we asked the Ouji for the identity of the perpetrators. The Ouji gave us the name of a neighbor. I became so fired up that I wanted to take matters into my own hands. Fortunately, I didn't. Years later, the real perpetrator was identified. We have to be very careful about the sources of our information.

While a preoccupation about uncovering memories can lead us

on an unproductive wild-goose chase and focus our attention upon the temporal instead of the comfort of the eternal, this is not to argue that God can't effectively confront us with our repressed material. He certainly can and seems to have done this very effectively with David following his adulterous behavior with Bathsheba and his murder of Uriah. David wrote:

> "When I kept silent, my bones grew old through my groaning all day long. For day and night Your hand was heavy upon me; my vitality was turned into the drought of the summer. I acknowledged my sin to You, and my iniquity I have not hidden. I said, 'I will confess my transgression to the Lord,' and You forgave the iniquity of my sin."[3]

This didn't happen all at once. David had perpetrated a giant cover-up and banished his sins into the nether world of his unconscious. He did keep hidden his 'iniquity' for a long time. It was only when the prophet Nathan, at God's instigation, confronted David with his sin through a story. He told David that a rich man with many sheep took the one sheep owned by a poor man. Nathan asked David what should be done to the rich man. David confidently replied that the rich man deserved to die. He had fallen into God's trap! Samuel then revealed to David that David was the transgressor in question. By God bringing the buried sin to David's attention, David confessed and repented. This is a far cry from strenuously hunting for our own repressed memories. Instead, we can trust God to reveal to us what He deems critical at just the right time.

This leads into the next danger of trying to uncover repressed material. The timing must be right. God had His own timing. Although the Bible doesn't specify the length of time, nor even why God waited as long as He did, it's obvious that understanding must be properly ordered. Forgiveness is only meaningful when it follows the acceptance of guilt. If I tell someone, "I forgive you," when he doesn't see what he has done wrong, he'll despise the insinuation that he's done something wrong. In David's case, he had to first see his own wretchedness. The prophet Nathan had done this by showing David that he was a thief and adulterer. David had also keenly suffered during the interval. He was now ready for a heart-to-heart with his Maker.

We can do a lot of harm by trying to force insights upon people when they aren't ready for them. Much of the reason that they don't have them themselves is that they *don't want* to have them. Our natural inclination is to run from the light. David didn't want the truth about himself. Circumstances had forced the truth upon him.

Sometimes we have to allow things to run their natural course without forcing them before their time. Only with disappointing results can we force a rosebud to open before its time. Forcing its delicate pedals can only ruin them.

Beyond the question of timing is the question of mental readiness. Are we mentally ready to meaningfully deal with the repressed material? We're the ones who had done the repressing in the first place. There were compelling reasons for us exert the kind of psychical energy needed to repress the material. There might still be compelling reasons that cause us to keep the material suppressed.

Shelley Taylor convincingly demonstrates that Homo sapiens don't want the truth about themselves but rather "creative self-deception." We prefer to feel good about self than to think rightly about self. One evidence of this is the fact that,

> "The evaluations people offer of themselves are also typically more favorable than judgments made by others about them...The perception of self that most people hold, then, is not as well balanced as traditional theories of mental health suggest."[4]

Only when people have acquired the readiness to deal with the painful repressed material can we rationally expect them to face it. David was able to face his adultery and murder because he believed that his God is merciful and would forgive him. How can we face our guilt squarely without the assurance of Divine forgiveness?

In my own life, there have been numerous failures that had been too painful to look at objectively. When I was about 12 years of age, four peers came to my house with a challenge. If I was really their friend, I'd loan them one of our two bikes for the forth youth, Louie, to pedal home on. That second bike belonged to my brother Gary. However, once Louie had pedaled the bike home along with the rest of us, we need some way to get the bike back to my home. It was Gary's bike, so he'd have to pedal it home. However, this meant that Gary would have to run along with us bike-less all the way to Louie's home in order to retrieve his bike. But these were my 'friends' and the thought of denying them the bike was unacceptable.

My compliant brother acquiesced without a word. I can still remember his tortured face as he desperately tried to keep pace with us from behind. Years later, this came up in a therapy session. My psychologist advised me to forgive myself. It had been a long time ago, and what I had done was a natural thing for a 12 year old. I tried this solution many times with diminishing results. I was left with my guilt and shame.

Could I have performed "self-forgiveness" more effectively? I don't think so. Self-affirmations have become the magic staff we wave over the painful flood of repressed memories to convert them into a gently flowing creek. "I am a good person. I try my best, although like everyone else, I sometimes make mistakes…I deserve the best…I have no right to punish myself." They work for a while but then lose their potency.

THE PROBLEM WITH SELF-AFFIRMATIONS AND SELF-ESTEEM

We have a certain nature which requires certain care. As we require certain foods for our sustenance, we also require certain psychical foods. Everything has a nature. When we buy a car, we receive a manual along with it, informing us about the proper upkeep of the vehicle. We have to put gasoline in the gas tank and water into the radiator and windshield fluid into its own depository. If we fail to treat a car in a way consistent with its nature it'll falter.

We too require treatment consistent with our nature. We require food, not gasoline, sleep and not an oil change.

The car also has a warning system to inform us when it's deviating from its normal functioning. It has an oil light that goes on and we might hear squeaking sounds when the breaks need changed. It might calm our anxiety to feed ourselves with the "positive affirmations" that "I've been through this type of thing before...I'm more than capable of dealing with any problem that arises...There is nothing to worry about...I can just put this little anxiety right out of my head." However, a more effective strategy would be to add oil, the sooner the better.

Often, a problem requires one particular solution. We have to understand our emotional problem, if we are going to deal with it appropriately. Some therapists advocate ignoring or assuaging the troublesome conscience rather than listening to its demands. This would be tantamount to taking a hammer to disable the oil light because we find its flashing worrisome.[5]

I needed to face the truth. I needed to be able to solidly confront the fact that I had hurt my brother without hiding behind the pile of excuses and affirmations which the psychotherapist had enabled me to employ. The problem was as real as the engine without oil. It wasn't enough to merely *acknowledge* that the engine was craving oil. It needed the actual oil! Likewise, it wasn't enough to merely acknowledge my guilt. The guilt had to be objectively dealt with. I needed to confess my guilt to my brother and to God.

There needs to be more acknowledgement of the fact that we're moral beings, and as such, we have certain requirements. Lawrence Kohlberg discovered that children across various cultures developed specific moral assessments at particular ages. This discovery is compatible with observations that we share such a common understanding of right and wrong irrespective of the upbringing and even the culture. Coming from such varied circumstances, only the existence of a common human nature is adequate to explain the common findings.

James Q. Wilson reasons that when we immediately respond

with sympathy or concern to the plight of others, it is not a product of intellectual reasoning, but a response that emanates from deep within the human psyche. It's not a matter of a decision but an "emotional reflex."[6]

When I was a college student, many were beginning to experiment with "open marriages." As a college student, I joined a sensitivity group. It soon became apparent that the leader was using the group as his hunting grounds for attractive venison. When one member confronted him with her observations, he admitted the whole thing. He explained that he and his wife were open to this type of thing as long as they conducted themselves in secret. It was workable as long as the other party was unaware of what was going on. I was surprised by what he subsequently confessed. He explained that they couldn't cope with knowing what was going on in his or his wife's sex life. Ask no questions, tell no lies. He admitted that on one occasion, he saw his wife entering the apartment of a suspected lover. He became so depressed that he had to be hospitalized! His problem wasn't that he had been raised without enough love and affection; his problem was that he had violated his nature. He had responded in a way that most of us would have responded.

In 1970, I was hunting for the ultimate utopian community among the Kibbutzim of Israel. The Kibbutz is an agricultural (at least at its inception) community where its residents share together in many of life's basic tasks. When they were initially founded in the twilight of the 20th century, most where rigorously socialistic. Although they had a democratic form of government where all have an equal voice, at least theoretically, everything else was shared. Coming from their strict socialistic, European background, they believed that all forms of ownership were oppressive. This included not only food and clothing, but also children and even spouses. There was a common laundry on many of the Kibbutzim. After the clothing was cleaned, the members freely pulled from the pile whatever clothing suited them for the next week. However, the sharing didn't stop there. Marriage too was regarded as an oppressive institution, a form of ownership. Consequently, at the inception of many of the Kibbutzim, no one was married. There was no wife swapping because there were no wives or even fixed couples. Likewise, the children were to belong to any particular father or mother. They were raised communally.

Although communal child rearing is still the norm on many kibbutzim, each child returns to his or her own parents after school for a traditional home experience. Husbands all claimed their respective wives and visa versa. Even their clothing has become their own although the communal dining hall still reigns. I knew of no instance where the 'open marriage' had prevailed as late as 1970, when I had arrived in Israel. Human nature had put an end to all such experimentation. It has certain requirements to which we must be responsive. Likewise, our repressed material can't always be adequately dealt with by positive self-talk. It has to be dealt with according to the laws of the soul.

Human nature has certain requirements. If this were not the case, we would find many sitting in corners happily fantasizing the ultimate relationship or accomplishment without any need to deal with the real world. Yes, we can do this, but only at the greatest expense to ourselves. In fact, we all do this in subtler ways. We inflate our self-estimation to artificial heights to feel good about ourselves. However, the "fix" is only temporary. Dr. Jennifer Crocker, a Psychologist at the University of Michigan's Institute of Social Research writes, "The pursuit of self-esteem has short-term benefits but long-term costs...ultimately diverting people from fulfilling their fundamental human needs."[7]

What are our human needs? Friendship, companionship, and sexual intimacy are qualifiers. As a TV show is no meaningful substitute for companionship, so too masturbation is a poor substitute for sexual intimacy. Might it also be that self-forgiveness is a poor and temporary substitute for Divine forgiveness? Simon Wiesenthal writes of a Nazi who, on his deathbed, asks a Jew, any Jew, for forgiveness. Self-forgiveness had clearly failed him. Our nature refuses to accept this as a legitimate substitute for the real thing. Self-affirmations have their limit.[8]

I still wince when I think back to Gary's pained face, but now I can laugh at my foolishness and my craving for peer acceptance. I have no image to maintain any longer nor any material I need to repress. I've come to terms with being a fool, but this is only because I've been given the wherewithal to handle what I've been repressing and denying. Without the assurance of a God who loves me just the way I am and without the sense of significance I receive from my Savior, I could never have faced the un-faceable. However, the problem of guilt first has to be dealt with objectively as we do in any relationship. We have to come to terms with it by humbling ourselves to confess it and to ask for forgiveness.

We not only repress guilt and shame but also an assortment of other painful material. However, the same principle still applies: if we lack the wherewithal to handle the material, it's best not to resurrect it. We suppress fears, humiliations, and pains. The secular answer generally involves talk, self-talk, and visualizations. John Bradshaw, writes of "redoing the old memory" through Neuro-Linguistic Programming (NLP). "I consider this (NLP) to be one of the most powerful for healing the shame that binds you."[9] It consists of "redoing the old memory" with memories of successful experiences that serve to refute and transform the painful memories or fears. In regards to NLP and other visualization techniques, he concludes, "These techniques are very powerful and will work whether you believe in them or not."[10]

How long will they work in the absence of solid evidence that our lives are indeed changed? Will we be able to successfully trust in these techniques as torrential fears continue to assault our lives? Aren't these mere secular substitutes for something far more powerful: trust in the living and performing God of the universe? These techniques might work admirably when pitted against irrational beliefs such as fearing to cross the George Washington Bridge lest it collapse as soon as we take a step upon it.

However, fear is often very appropriate. How can we not be overwhelmed by it when we see that we are vulnerable to so many painful things and ultimately death? NLP harkens back upon trusting self. We derive a lift-me-up by visualizing ourselves as competent and successful. However, we know in truth that we can't guarantee any positive outcome for ourselves. It's just not in our power! If we are truthful with ourselves, we have to admit that the security and peace that we seek must be found in Another.

Rather than facing the truth about ourselves and our repressed material, this can represent the ultimate avoidance of the light in an attempt to create an alternative vision. Visualizing self and trusting in self had led to years of crippling and blinding depression. Although this form of self-stimulation can lead to temporary successes, ultimately it further commits us to the psychological death of self-obsession. If trust has self as its object, then self becomes our sanctuary. Do we really want to place such a weight upon our shoulders?

The diagnoses of traditional therapies are often too shallow and their solutions too inadequate. I'll use depression as an example. It is widely understood that depressive thinking is characterized by negativity and negative self-assessments. Aaron Beck claims that "depression is the consequence of false logic, and that by correcting negative reasoning one may achieve better mental health."[11] Thinking determines how we feel and react to the world. Intervention involves confrontation of these beliefs to demonstrate that they're neither reasonable nor helpful. Sometimes the therapist will try to show how negative thinking finds its origin in the context of a strict, non-accepting household. The hope is that the patient will then see that their beliefs and thinking are arbitrary and not truth-based.

Our readiness to see depression as pathology and non-depression as normal has served to impede understanding the phenomenon. Andrew Solomon writes, "Non-depressed people invariably believe themselves to have more control than they really have, and depressed people give an accurate assessment. In a study done with a video game, depressed people who played for a half an hour knew just how many little monsters they had killed; the undepressed people guessed four to six times more than they had actually hit."[12]

This type of finding isn't unusual and should cause us to reassess what is sickness and what is normalcy. It should also caution us about our concept of therapy. Solomon maintains that Freud "observed that the melancholic has 'a keener eye for the truth than others who are not melancholic'." How can this be if the depressed are the mentally ill?

It would seem that if the depressed are in some sense ill, then so too is everyone else. Everyone suffers from some problem. Either one is depressed or one is deluded. Shelley Taylor offers one possible solution. Taylor argues that illusions are really positive and necessary as long as they don't go too far. Therefore, illusions are the best we can hope for, and absolute truth isn't good for mental health.

Seeing this, Solomon concludes, "Life is futile...Depressives have seen the world too clearly, have lost the selective advantage of blindness."[13] If he's correct, then all of this discussion about the therapeutic enterprise is also futile. This, however, is too fatalistic for most of us. There must an "underground railroad" to freedom, a way of escape from the dilemma. Meanwhile, how is it that the entire human race falls prey to this futility?

A CHRISTIAN ALTERNATIVE

Christian assessment has to acknowledge two things. Firstly, humankind has a real and objective problem whether a person is clinically depressed or happy. Shame, guilt, jealousy, and a myriad of other afflictions are not merely happenchance feelings arbitrarily communicated to children by dysfunctional parents who themselves had dysfunctional parents. Instead, they are part of a larger, universal narrative reflecting an initial "big bang" when God's Word was spurned and He was rejected. Although the human race removed themselves from God, they failed to remove themselves from His laws and truths written upon their hearts.[14] Consequently, we have been trying to regain our lost original righteousness ever since. This is manifested in our pursuit of success, accomplishment, respect, virtue and intimacy so that we can feel adequate within ourselves.

Not that there is anything wrong with these things within themselves, but lacking the original relationship with God, these things have become a substitute form of worth and self-image. The unconscious is the receptacle for all manner of repressed thoughts. Is it any wonder that we also repress the knowledge of our rejection of God? To face it means we must do something about it.

Secondly, if there's a real and objective problem based upon the disruption of our relationship with God, then there must be a real and objective solution that directly answers this problem. It's not enough to merely confront the problem of our guilt and shame embedded within our repressed memories. It's not enough to merely smooth the rough edges over with the magic wand of creative visualizations and positive self-affirmations. There's an underlying problem that must be addressed. Yes, to a certain degree we can recreate ourselves through thinking, will, and lots of elbow grease. However, certain problems require much more than creativity. There has to be an accurate accounting of the problem and an evaluation of various solutions. If you have a hole in your boat, no amount of talk therapy, visualizations, or positive affirmations is going to do the trick.

Since our intimate relationship with God had been fractured, we seek after the worth and significance that had originally come from Him. We all need to feel valued, respected, and loved. We try to achieve these things through fulfilling the moral standards placed by God within our hearts.[15] Performance becomes key. Whereas relationship was central and performance was a fruit of that relationship, now relationship has become a product of performance. We attempt to become worthy of love, even our own love and approval. We don't seem to have the ability to sit in a corner to merely conjure up visions of worth and significance without paying a high price for our delusions. We have to achieve in the social arena.

What happens when we fail to meet performance expectations?—Shame and guilt! (We can never fulfill these expectations. We can never say we've arrived. Every day has a full set of demanding requirements.) It seems that we have three ways to deal with these painful, controlling feelings. Repression is the quickest.

We merely push the failures and pains out of our mind. However, we find that our attempts are less than adequate. What we repress continues to invade our conscious life.

A more effective and involved strategy involves rationalization, relaxation, and redefinition of the standards. We do this to convince ourselves of our own righteousness, deservedness, and worth. We make excuses for our all too obvious failures: "No one can be perfect," "I'm a better person than 95% of the others," "God knows, I'm a good person." There is no way to exhaust all of our rationalizations. Whenever we engage in ego-inflation, we are rationalizing in order to both avoid the guilt and shame and to exalt self above others. This is the way of self-righteousness. We avoid our own absolute, God-ingrained standards in favor of a relative standard by which we convince ourselves that we're better than others.

A more honest response is that of blame. We intuitively know that there's a price to pay and someone must pay it.[16] Of course, it's easier to blame someone else, but we soon learn that this incurs the wrath of others. Those who are blamed generally don't stand still for it. We can also blame ourselves. This makes the most sense. We were the ones who failed our own standards. We deserve the blame. This, however, is the most painful solution. We vow to try harder and do better. We grit our teeth and march against the enemy trenches. This way may produce fruit for a while, as long as success lasts. However, if we're honest with ourselves, we recognize that we inevitably fall far short of our standards. As we're defeated time after time, blame increases and without an adequate way to deal with it, so too depression and despair.

From God's perspective, depression is no worse than repression and avoidance or the "normal" response of self-righteousness and inflated self-esteem. They all fail to confront the real problem. However, if someone murdered his wife, depression might be construed as the more appropriate response of the three. In such an extreme case, most of us would deem grotesque any consolation found in positive affirmations. Most would insist that the guilty party face the enormity of what he had done. Should it be any different for we who have rejected our Creator and Redeemer?

Where there is a real and objective problem, there must also be an objective solution that addresses the problem. If the problem is violation and rejection of God, then the solution must be confession and reception of the dethroned Potentate. The rejected husband isn't going to be cheered to hear that his wife is finding peace and contentment either through repression of her guilt or through positive self-affirmations: "I'm really a good person…Anyone has a right to be happy…I've suffered enough…"

Adam and Eve disobeyed God's law by eating from the "tree of the knowledge of good and evil" and rejected Him. Immediately, knowing they had violated, they were overcome by guilt and shame. Their sense of innocence and righteousness was fractured. Nakedness had never been a problem before, but now their shame made their nakedness intolerable. Why should shame affix to nakedness? Nakedness is equivalent to exposure, the very thing that shame dreads. When we're ashamed of ourselves, we don't want anyone to see us.

Therefore, their first response was to remove the nakedness or shame so it couldn't be seen. They sewed fig leaves together to suppress the shame. This is generally our first response. Hide the problem; make believe it doesn't exist. However, this rarely suffices, so we resort to more comprehensive means. The couple hid from God. As unreasonable as this might seem to us, repression or avoidance is equally unreasonable. We put our head in the sand and hope the problem will just disappear.

Nevertheless, God found the desperate couple and asked, "Where are you?" Rather than jumping upon them with an outstretched accusing finger, God gave them room to confess what they had done. Seeing that avoidance failed to work, they shifted to the strategy of self-justification or rationalization.

"I heard Your voice in the garden, and I was afraid because I was naked; and I hid myself."[17] They had every reason to hide. After all, they were naked, and who wants to be seen when they're naked. According to Adam, their behavior was unimpeachable. In other words, "Why shouldn't I hide? This nakedness is unbearable!" Notice that self-justification fails to deal with the real problem of the violation of both God and His law. It fails to come to terms with reality by admitting wrongdoing. In addition to this, Adam seemed to insinuate that he was justified because it was God's faultfinding 'voice' which had caused them to fear. Besides, God had never given them clothing; that's why they were naked!

God then brought the conversation back to the real issue. "Who told you that you were naked? Have you eaten from the tree of which I commanded you that you should not eat?"[18] Again, they were given a chance to confess their guilt and to plead for mercy. Nevertheless, they clung to their original strategy to establish their righteousness to counteract the insinuations of guilt and shame.

Then the man said, "The woman whom *You* gave to be with me, she gave me of the tree, and I ate."[19] Adam was the righteous one. It was Eve who was at fault and even God who gave her to Adam. This is the nucleus of self-righteousness: a rejection of God and His righteousness and a promotion of our own through avoidance and self-deception. If we are going to oppose the accusations that threaten our well being, we have to establish our own righteousness or worthiness. Adam and Eve eventually succeeded in removing this guilt-seeking God from their presence, but they failed to remove the law from their heart into which it had been built. Left alone with an accusing heart, they had committed psychological suicide. Now separated from their intimate relationship with God, they had condemned themselves to the self-obsession. They would now endlessly try to prove themselves both to the world and to themselves through their accomplishments, positive self-talk, and whatever tools they would have at their disposal.

For some reason, rationalization, avoidance, and blaming others don't suffice for the depressed. They endure their own accusations of failure all alone. It should therefore be no surprise that self-talk and visualizations also fail to suffice. They require what the rest of us ultimately require: a true acceptance of guilt and shame based upon our transgressions. The problem is a real one; it's also a relational one. An offended party must be satisfied, and nothing short of a full confession will do it. If I ruin someone's reputation through gossip, no amount of payment or good deeds will suffice apart from a humble confession. Everything else is superficial.

While Adam blamed Eve and God, Eve blamed the serpent. Neither uttered a word of sorrow, let alone confession. They made a decision that has been endlessly recapitulated throughout the course of human history. Humankind have uniformly hungered after their lost sense of righteousness and completeness as they've struggled to cover their shame and guilt with the fig leaves of success, respect, and human relationships which have failed to endure the expectations placed upon them.

Self-castigation also fails. God provided a better way. He loves us so much that He doesn't want us to punish ourselves. Instead, He took the punishment upon Himself that anyone who will open his or her eyes to His truth shall be saved.

All of this might help us to understand Christianity's track record. Patrick Glynn was an atheist. However, after assessing the evidence for God, he committed himself to Christianity. He investigated recent therapeutic findings regarding American churchgoers. Here are some of his findings.

1. "Persons who did not attend church were four times as likely to commit suicide than were frequent church attendees. A review of twelve studies of the relationship between church commitment and suicide found a negative correlation in all twelve cases."
2. "One survey of nearly 14,000 youths found...the most conservative religious youth abusing least."
3. "Several studies have found that a high level of religious commitment correlate with lower levels of depression,...stress."[20]

Glynn cites the same kinds of findings for various other concerns like divorce, marital and sexual satisfaction, and overall happiness and psychological well-being. He concludes, "Modern research in psychology makes clear that the morally unrestrained life is not worth living."[21]

Primitive peoples have long intuited the problem and have

known that the ultimate answer lied outside of their flimsy grasp. They made continuous offerings to gods who abused, possessed, and enslaved them with fear. Jungleman, a Yanomamo Shaman: states, "I wish I had known the truth about Yai Wana Naba Laywa (God) when I was a young man—it would have saved me so much pain and misery. But how could I? My spirits lied so much to me and tricked me. They were so beautiful, so wonderful, so hard not to want…Now I'm at the end of this life, and I'm ready to begin my real life with Yai Pada (God)."[22]

EXERCISE

1. Have you ever confronted repressed material? Were you able to deal with it meaningfully? How?

2. Was timing a factor?

3. What tools or understandings are necessary for successfully processing repressed material?

4. In what ways does a faulty understanding of human nature hurt others? hurt society in general?

5. Do we serve our own best interests by following the 'manual'?

---

[1] Opening Skinner's Box, Lauren Slater, W.W. Norton and Company, 2004, pg.191.

[2] Ibid.

[3] Psalm 32:3-5

[4] Positive Illusions, Shelley Taylor, Basic Books, Inc., NY, NY, 1986, pg. 11.

[5] This doesn't mean that the conscience always preaches the "Gospel truth." But it does suggest that we have to evaluate the signal it's emitting. However, this evaluation requires much sobriety and moral sensibilities that are often lacking.

[6] The Moral Sense, James Q. Wilson, Free Press Paperbacks, NY, NY, 1997, pg. 8.

[7] "Deflating Self-Esteem's Role in Society's Ills," Erica Goode, New York Times, 10/1/02.

[8] Sunflower

[9] Healing the Shame that Binds You, John Bradshaw, Health Communications, Inc., Deerfield Beach, Fla., 1988, pg. 172.

[10] Ibid., pg. 181.

[11] The Noonday Demon: An Atlas of Depression, Andrew Solomon, Scribner, NY, NY, 2001, pg. 107.

[12] Ibid., pg. 433.

[13] Ibid., pg. 434.

[14] Romans 2:15

[15] We should do this, but for the *right* reasons. Good deeds are important, but if we use them as a basis to establish God's indebtedness to us, we use them illegitimately.

[16] Romans 1:32

[17] Genesis 3:10

[18] Gen. 3:11

[19] Gen. 3:12

[20] God: The Evidence, Patrick Glynn, Rocklin, Ca., 1999, pgs. 63-65.

[21] Ibid. pg. 77.

[22] Spirit of the Rainforest, Mark Andrew Ritchie, Island Lake Press, Chicago, 1989, pg. 238.

CHAPTER 14

Psychotherapy, the Past and Christianity

> Wisdom is the principal thing. Therefore get wisdom. And in all your getting, get understanding. Exalt her, and she will promote you; she will bring you honor, when you embrace her. **Proverbs 4:7-8**

So many of us are sold on the idea that understanding our past translates into a cure from present hurts and disabilities. Because of this, we invest great sums of money, effort, and hope into trying to understand those influences that made us the way we are today, convinced that this will bring freedom. Understanding is truly valuable, but we may be erroneously placing our hope and efforts into the pursuit of an unfruitful form of understanding.

A critical distinction has to be made. Meaningful self-awareness does not necessarily depend upon understanding how we *became* the way we are. I've learned from past experience that if I tie my shoe too tightly, I can cause myself considerable pain. Although I don't understand the mechanism of pain or even why I have this problem and others don't, this knowledge is still valuable. We've all learned through past experience that certain people can't be trusted and that avoidance might be a wise course of action. We might not know why they are untrustworthy, but it's enough to know that they can cause us considerable discomfort.

Knowing our past can be very helpful. We all need to get a grip upon who we are—how we act, how we affect others, and how we see life through distorted lenses. In the movie, "A Beautiful Mind," Russell Crow played a brilliant but schizophrenic mathematician. He believed that his self-aggrandizing hallucinations were reality. These led him to a complete breakdown. Recovery required that he realize that what he had seen wasn't reality and that it had led to his breakdown. Armed with this understanding, he was able to oppose and discount the hallucinations and to fight his way back into reality and functionality.

It wasn't essential that Crow came to understand what had initially made him schizophrenic. He didn't require knowledge of genetics or brain chemistry. Nor was it essential that he obtain accurate knowledge of other schizophrenics in his family tree, nor what medications his mother was using during her pregnancy. What was critical was to recognize his hallucinogenic patterns and to realize that they were no more than hallucinations.

John Modrow explains it was critical for him to be objectively shown that he wasn't a prophet, as he had believed. He had been confronted with incontrovertible evidence. Fortunately, he hadn't believed in his prophetic abilities for a long period of time.

His recovery from schizophrenic hallucination was the product not of understanding the developmental stages that he went through to become a schizophrenic but rather a recognition that his delusions didn't reflect reality. Subsequently, Modrow was able to identify developmental circumstances that had driven him in the direction of Schizophrenia.[1] However, even if he is correct about these causal agents, this knowledge will not enable him to undo his problem. But they may be valuable in helping other families avoid that road.

There is a critical difference between understanding who we are by reflecting upon our past, and understanding developmental factors. These latter factors are far more complex and possess

178

uncertain therapeutic value. Growth largely depends upon the former than upon the factors that formed us, although the former might require that we take note of historical patterns of thought and conduct in order to understand our present tendencies.

Sometimes knowledge is power. I was empowered to manage my feet more profitably by understanding what caused me pain. If I know how to drive a car, I can get some chores done and maybe even make some money. But sometimes knowledge doesn't translate into power or advantage. I might know the chemical composition of newspaper ink, but this won't help me understand the newspaper or even publish one. I might understand biologically what happened when a shark bit off my leg, but this won't help me grow a new one or even to live without one. (I do have two legs!)

More to the point, when I look back over my life, I see certain patterns. As far back as I can remember, I had a strong tendency to anticipate rejection. As a result, I would reject others before they had an opportunity to reject me. I also recognize that this has caused needless pain. As a result of recognizing my skewed way of seeing things and that I wasn't seeing reality as I should have, I can now make certain adjustments. I can remind myself that my feelings don't necessarily reflect the reality of the relationship. Such knowledge allows me to exert meaningful control over my life. Having this type of knowledge, I might seek some objective feedback about what my feelings are telling me. Knowledge of developmental factors however is not only more tenuous, it doesn't appear to be therapeutically fruitful, at least for the sufferer.

I certainly have ideas about why I've been so sensitive to rejection, but I might be wrong. It might be a human thing. No one enjoys rejection. Perhaps it was accentuated by my experience as a Jew on the margins of school and community life? Perhaps original sin is contributory? Perhaps a sensitivity to rejection is something I learned from my parents or even grandparents? Perhaps it's the result of 50 factors? However, this question isn't critical to my growth. What is critical is that I know that it's not right to hurt others by rejecting them, and that I'm quick on the rejection trigger. Looking deeper, it was important to recognize that my rejection of others was always associated with a fear that they'd reject me first. This enabled me to become suspect of my feelings, before I'd come to any conclusions, and to correct the way that I was seeing things. However, none of these insights freed me from the feelings, although they mitigated my reaction to them. When I realize that people aren't rejecting me, my angry reaction is quieted. Even if I did have perfect understanding of the developmental factors responsible for my feelings, there's no reason to expect that it would banish my distorted feelings any more than understanding the shark's motivations for biting my leg off will restore my leg.

Knowledge of my past is also important for the purpose of assigning culpability. Recognizing my past pattern of rejection, I've tried to correct some of my relationships by admitting my guilt. Sometimes it's healing for both parties, sometimes not. Anita and I have been restored on so many occasions because I reexamined my behavior and confessed my guilt to her. The same pertains to our relationship with God. Recognizing our past guilt before God brings us to heaven's gate.

A prostitute had come to Jesus; she cried over his feet, washing his feet with her tears and anointing them with precious oil. Jesus explained to His incredulous watchers that because she had understood the enormity of her guilt and the forgiveness she had received, her love transcended all bounds.[2]

We need to be reconciled to the God we've rejected and offended all our lives. Reconciliation is impossible without recognition and confession of our guilt.[3]

David also drew critical truths from the knowledge of his past behavior of adultery and murder. He writes,

> "When I kept silent, my bones grew old through my groaning all the day long. For day and night Your hand was heavy upon me; my vitality was turned into the drought of summer. I acknowledged my sin to You, and my iniquity I have not hidden. I said, 'I will confess my transgressions to the Lord,' and You forgave the iniquity of my sin."[4]

David examined his past behavior and drew from it some critical lessons. He learned that sin could cause somatic suffering. He learned that God forgives sin, even the most heinous. He was renewed in the knowledge that there's no substitute for prayer and the forgiveness of God.

Knowledge of the past serves many useful functions, but is it important to understand how our various past influences have determined our present mental health status? Larry Crabb has his doubts. He writes, "The further we move away from things and toward people, the less useful explanations become."[5] Crabb sees healing taking place in the context of Christian relationships and eschews the therapeutic importance of explanations and cathartic events. Crabb asserts, "the soul can be studied but never explained; nourished but not possessed; influenced by many forces outside of itself, but never fully predicted."[6]

Crabb cautions, "The demand to know what's causing our difficulties may actually be preventing us from finding a pathway through them to joy."[7] This has been my experience. The focus upon psychopathology and its preoccupation with finding explanations runs several risks. Firstly, it invites the sufferer to adopt the "disease mentality." This can be quite degrading. We begin to see that almost everything we think and feel is a product of the disease and our circuitous attempts to escape it. Seeking the good or the noble is reduced to a neurotic attempt to feel good about ourselves. We do good to others because we want them to like us. We speak the truth because we want respect. There is no longer anything noble, honorable, or even brave. It all about the pathology, and we are that pathology.

Secondly, this focus upon causation and pathology tends to isolate. My past and pathology are distinctively my own. It's an unwanted disease and a source of shame. I'm not only going to want to distance myself from it but also from others who I perceive to share it. If it's something that I can't accept about myself, then I will not accept its presence in others. In contrast with this perspective is the focus upon our common human nature, something with which we all struggle. For instance, we all seek recognition, worth, and significance. We can laugh and cry about it together, compare notes and share what we've learned. I know what you're thinking and you know what I'm thinking. I don't have to feel so ashamed about my struggles because they're not so different from yours. I think that this is one of the strengths of the twelve step programs. They emphasize the fact that we're all together. All are powerless; all need a Higher Power; all have to follow the same program of recovery despite the personal differences.

Thirdly, as Crabb pointed out, seeking explanations may keep us from real solutions, namely looking towards the Source of all of our hope and help. In conjunction with this, self-focus can cause depression to snowball downward. We look at our thoughts and feelings and obsess, "Why am I feeling this way? Why can't I climb out of this? What's the matter with me that I'm so helpless?" As we begin to feel even worse through entertaining these thoughts, our thoughts become correspondingly worse, then the feelings worsen, etc. If all we have is our diseased selves to trust in for recovery, what hope can we possibly have? We've failed ourselves for years. Why suddenly should we think that things will now be otherwise?

Fourthly, among those who claim to have found relief in finding out why they are a certain way, there remain critical questions. Did they come to the right explanation? Would any explanation have sufficed? One of my students experienced relief in merely being told that she was depressed. She needed an explanation, any explanation. Although a label can stigmatize, a label can also put to rest the obsessive question, "What's happening to me?" A label can also serve to place the blame elsewhere, perhaps erroneously.

Lastly, there's no logical connection between understanding developmental influences and relief from its effects. Even if I come to understand why Bill shot me in the back, it's not going to restore my spinal cord. Yes, many people claim to have been helped through this type of therapy. But what exactly is it that has helped them? Many therapists regard the client relationship as the most critical part of therapy. Through the relationship, the client can unburden himself and experience affirmation in their most hurting parts. However, this isn't always a plus. Often we profit more from confrontation and not affirmation. One-on-one psychotherapy has been often found counterproductive in sexual abuse and domestic violence cases. As a supervisor for a unit of Probation Officers who supervised these specific cases, I saw this firsthand. The manipulative perpetrators had been consistently able to co-opt the therapist into accepting his own point of view at the expense of the unseen victim. This has a tendency of reinforcing the criminal behavior. The courts also became aware of this sad reality and subsequently required that the criminal attend group programs, which are confrontational and have a strong educational component.

Many attribute psychotherapeutic success to growth in self-esteem rather than to understanding developmental factors. Psychotherapy has become so eclectic, that, more often than not, some form of self-esteem promotion has become a part of insight therapy. Although this remedy is pandered to a variety of sufferers including the depressed, prisoners, underachiever students, and the obese. However, experimental findings haven't been reassuring. Failure hasn't been found to be directly associated with low self-esteem. Erica Goode writes, " 'D' students think as highly of themselves as valedictorians, and serial rapists are no more likely to ooze with insecurities than doctors or bank managers."[8] Furthermore, there's no reason to believe that by raising self-esteem societies ills will be mitigated or that psychological healing will result. Goode adds, "High self-esteem, studies show, offers no immunity against bad behavior." Citing research by Bushman and Baumeister, she writes, "Some people with high self-esteem are actually more likely to lash out aggressively when criticized than those with low self esteem."

Citing an extensive review of studies, she writes that Nicholas Emler "found no clear link between low self-esteem and delinquency, violence against others, teenage smoking, drug use, or racism…High self-esteem, on the other hand, was positively correlated with racist attitudes, drunken driving and other risky behaviors."

In many cases, the benefit that is seen to accrue to a positive self-esteem is only temporary. Quoting Dr. Jennifer Crocker she writes, "The pursuit of self-esteem has short term benefits but long term costs...ultimately diverting people from fulfilling their fundamental human needs for competence, relatedness and autonomy and leading to poor self-regulation and mental and physical health." Crocker contrasts students who sought their self-worth in external performance with those "who judged themselves by more internal measures like virtue or religious faith who seemed to fair better. They were less likely to show anger and aggression and more restrained in their use of alcohol and drugs." This suggests that we look with caution upon therapeutic successes based upon improvement in self-esteem. Bitter fruits might be the eventual harvest.

The Bible often points us to the broader perspective, warning that a limited picture may prove very misleading. Jesus talks about someone who builds a respectable house, but it's one built upon the sand of self-righteousness. It's an enviable house until a storm comes.[9] He also makes reference to someone freed from demonic influence without also being reconciled to the Divine. Although his status seems much improved, it's only temporary. His house now swept clean, he has become doubly vulnerable to a much worse demonic assault.[10] This might parallel the fate of those who find temporary benefit through self-inflation. Those who exalt themselves shall be humbled.

Quoting an article published by the American Psychological Association in "Psychology Review," which analyzed 150 studies, Bernard Bauer writes, "The societal pursuit of high self-esteem for everyone may literally end up doing considerable harm." He elaborates, "They found aggressive people have unusually high self-esteem—defined as 'a favorable global evaluation of oneself'—especially compared to achievements...The study found that aggressive, violent and hostile people—such as neo-Nazis, wife-beaters and members of the Klu Klux Klan—'consistently express favorable views of themselves.'"[11]

This leads us to one last question about the validity of client "self-reports" of therapeutic progress. Does secular counseling, in its heavy reliance upon self-esteem promotion, produce overall benefit to society in general? Does it enable one to lead a more violent or selfish life? What is the net result for a society when a high percentage of its members undergo this form of therapy? Although it's difficult to weigh its overall impact, the question is certainly relevant.

A CHRISTIAN PERSPECTIVE

Christianity has always placed more emphasis upon identifying our own personal guilt than in pointing the guilty finger. The same applies to the question of therapy and understanding our past. The best therapy is a penitent spirit whether it's repentant about past decisions or present behaviors. It's the broken and contrite heart that elicits the mercy of God.[12]

Today, we have such a different orientation towards our past. We try to understand ourselves through the lens of *external* developmental influences. Reading Augustine's Confessions helped me become aware of a radically different perspective. Augustine confessed sins we'd regard as miniscule, and he took complete responsibility for them, never once attributing his proclivity or behavior to anyone else. He could easily have done otherwise. He had an abuser as a father. Augustine labored for almost a chapter trying to come to terms with the full extent of his guilt for needlessly stealing pears only to discard them.

Likewise, David, in his zeal to make a full confession of sin stated hyperbolically that he "was conceived in sin."[13] Rather than pushing his sin off upon his parents, he acknowledged that he was a sinner from his conception.

In the spirit of Augustine, I'd like to argue that we're guiltier than we have supposed, and by acknowledging this guilt, we can realize a greater measure of grace. Habits exert a powerful impact upon our lives. I've struggled for years trying to change my nail-biting habit whose foundation had been laid in the obscure recesses of the past. Many of us have waged war against nicotine and caffeine addiction. Some habits are worse than others. They commandeer more of our lives, circumscribing our freedom of thought and of movement. Just ask a heroin addict who has resorted to a methadone maintenance program. Some addictions are life controlling. We are unaware of many of our addictions and habits. They form the underlying grid for our thinking and feeling that's largely invisible to us. But we know that this grid exists. It must! We recognize that we respond to certain circumstances in a habitual, knee-jerk manner.

Where do the habits come from? They aren't merely *instilled* from the outside, but often it's our early *choices* that are pivotal as is the case with any habit formation. As heroin is a choice producing a life-controlling addiction, is it likely that our life-controlling habits are also the result of our early choices? When I was 12 years old, I transferred to the Junior High School some distance from my home and outside of my somewhat Jewish neighborhood. There I began to encounter a lot of scorn and hatred by virtue of my Jewish identity. It was easy for my assailants to determine who was Jewish. In my pre-Bar Mitzvah years, our school would make announcements over the loud speaker system for the Jewish students to line up in preparation for the bus that would take us to Hebrew school twice weekly. I dreaded these times. They would always be accompanied by laughter and derision. The other Jewish students never said anything. They never seemed to care. I felt that I alone was pierced by humiliation.

I determined that I'd have my revenge. I would slay them in the privacy of my heart. They were less than garbage to me. I fancied that they were all Christians. I was sure that they all had a Christmas tree and that of course made them Christians. If you were born to Jewish parents, you were Jewish. If you were born to parents who had a Christmas tree, you were Christian. It was that easy.

Later, I realized other things about these hated "Christians." I was sure that they all hated Jews. I had seen Gentile youth, whom I had trusted, turn against me when the name-calling began. That was proof-positive that they all hated Jews. Even the teachers hated

186

Jews. They never seemed to intervene when Jews were being bullied.

I began to also realize that all the Gentiles had a different odor. Of course, it was a putrid odor. It became difficult for me to be around them in close quarters. But this didn't represent any sacrifice for me. I had since learned to mistrust anyone who wasn't Jewish and kept my distance. Elevators were particularly difficult. I had a good friend, Jewish of course, who had joined a basketball league, something that Jews didn't do. Except for him, it was entirely Gentile, and they played at a YMCA. He invited me to one of his games. I didn't want to go, but he was a good friend. I because nauseated by the smell of mildew that issued up from the lockers below, but I knew that this was the smell of 'Christians'. It wasn't until my college years at Berkeley in the mid-sixties that I began to reassess some of my assumptions. I'm sure my Gentile girlfriend had a big impact.

My early and sinful commitment to hate exercised a strong influence upon my subsequent development and response formation, but it wasn't a decision made in a vacuum. There had been prior, sinful decisions that had inclined me in this direction. When I was seven years old, I would recite my prayers including the Lord's Prayer and the 23rd Psalm every evening, with hands reverently clasped together, upon getting into bed. This was nothing I had learned within my own family. In those years, prayers were still being offered in the public schools. This included the recitation of the Lord's Prayer and the 23rd Psalm. I didn't know that Jews didn't do this type of thing.

However, I remember that several of my youthful prayers were answered. I had heard the adults talking in hushed tones that Uncle Jack was going to die within days. I set about praying for him and he lived for another 15 years. Nevertheless, at the mature year of eight, I came to realize that I was Jewish and that what I was doing was improper. I quickly ceased performing my nocturnal ritual. Consequently, I stopped praying entirely, not just in the Christian mode. I had placed ethnic identification above truth, a choice that would continue to exercise profound effects over my unhappy life.

I'm aware that to many of my readers, my interpretation of these stories is offensive. I'm taking responsibility for my developmental choices and the resulting negative consequences. Many will feel that the blame should be placed upon external factors, especially upon anti-Semitism. I don't deny this. Anti-Semitism *also* is to blame. However, my primary focus before God is what I've done wrong. This is the primary place where I can make an impact, especially in terms of my relationship with God.

Hate is primarily a sin against God, the Source of all moral truth. When I hate, I'm telling God, "My way is better than yours. I have no obligation to follow Your ways." I am duty bound to confess this sin to God who wants us to be scrupulously honest with ourselves.[14]

Although anti-Semites are blameworthy, I can't blame them for *my* sin. I could have responded differently. Perhaps this would have been difficult for me, but the choice was still mine, a choice that proved to have profound consequences. I've made other sinful choices. At an early age, I determined that I was going to be the best at anything that I did. This too had negatives consequences. It's one thing to try to be as good as one can be; it's another thing to decide to be better than anyone else, lustily demanding within myself to have everything that others had. Such a choice proved a prescription for misery. It was impossible to be the best at everything. Any setback was an occasion for discontent, bitterness and envy. I would never concede that others deserved the acclaim that they had received. The wheels I had set in motion, I couldn't stop nor even see.

I can blame my pursuit for self-aggrandizement upon childhood deprivations, but I won't. I've consistently found that confession of sin, even in the face of victimization, is healing. It brings me into intimate contact with Christ. Perhaps, this is because He too forgave His persecutors.

One can argue that I lacked the maturity to make any other choice than the one I had made. However, the case would be difficult to make. As an eight year old, I chose ethnic identification over a relationship with God. I don't remember why I had made such a choice, but I certainly can't claim complete ignorance. I had seen God answer the hopeful prayers of a seven year old. I thanked Him for it and felt comfort in the fact that I could turn to Him.

Perhaps the heroin addict now can't stop on his own. Nevertheless, even if this is the case, he is clearly culpable for picking up the drug in the first place. Had I not rejected God as an eight year old, I would have had a Counselor to advise me otherwise. I reaped the consequences of my early choice.

We can regard ourselves as a product of our past or as a major player. I'm convinced that the "choice" perspective is a significant one for growth. More is to be gained by acknowledging our faults than by placing the blame upon someone or something else. Friends have accused me of engaging in self-punishment. Instead, my practice is one of self-interest. I just know how important it is to have a broken and tender conscience before the Lord. This is the avenue to God's mercy and peace, to not minimize our sin but to confess it in all its ugliness.

> "People who cover over their sins will not prosper. But if they confess and forsake them, they will receive mercy. Blessed are those who have a tender conscience, but the stubborn are headed for serious trouble."[15]

Not only must we see ourselves as a major player, it's important to see our struggles globally. We're trained to see mental conflict and failure as negatives, things to be hidden at all costs. From the micro- perspective they are negatives! However, from a Biblical perspective, they can also serve as opportunities. Peter taught that Christians would have to experience the sufferings Christ did.[16] Paul talked about the privilege of participating in the same sufferings as Christ. Jesus used the example of a prostitute to teach an important spiritual lesson. Knowing that she had been forgiven, she reciprocated Jesus' love by washing His feet with her tears. Through this, Jesus taught his rich and powerful, yet appalled hosts that those who are forgiven much will also love much.[17] Knowledge of her sin became her doorway into blessedness.

Christianity doesn't deny the importance of developmental causation. The Bible contains a lot of wisdom regarding raising children and the importance of early training. However, Christianity understands these factors as only part of our life narrative. The prostitute had most likely emerged from a difficult childhood. Consequently, despite its social unacceptability, she entered a life-sucking profession that would eventually break her and deprive her of any self-respect. However, in this broken and humbled state, she thrust herself down upon the mercy of God to discover forgiveness and a love that would transform her.

It seems that Martin Luther had come from a family where he couldn't please his demanding parents and also felt that he could never be righteous enough to please God. There was no lack of effort. He wrote that on several occasions he had almost died because he pursued his spiritual disciplines so rigorously. Failing to find relief from his guilt and fear, he resorted to confession daily for hours. However, when he came to understand grace, he embraced it more fervently than anyone else. From the context of his personal darkness, God's grace shined all the more brilliantly. This bright light not only illuminated his own life, but it sparked the most profound "back to the Bible" movement in history.

If we only see Luther's psychopathology in its narrow context, our understanding of growth will not only be limited but also greatly distorted. The micro-narrative is important but only in as far as it serves the macro-narrative. Winston Churchill was one of the most important figures of the 20th century. Lacking the intimate love of both mother and father, Churchill compensated through dreams of great attainment. He determined that he was going to be a Member of Parliament and eventually Prime Minister. It was his "pathology" that constituted the greatest single factor for the defeat of Nazism.

From this lofty perspective, we should recognize that our pathologies are only of secondary importance, if that. This is because there is a God who doesn't place importance upon the narrow estimation of humankind, nor is He confined by our limited perspectives.

"All the inhabitants of the earth are reputed as nothing; He does according to His will in the army of heaven and among the inhabitants of the earth. No one can restrain His hand or say to Him, 'What have You done?'"[18]

In addition to this, there is nothing that prevents Him from taking a negative and using it to accomplish grand purposes. Indeed, He delights in taking hopeless prostitutes and clothing them in beauty.

EXERCISE

1. Have you noticed how the way you understand and conceptualize life and its struggles affects the types of solutions to which you gravitate?

2. What are the implications of having one paradigm as opposed to another? Which have you found most productive?

3. Have you become more aware of your habits or patterns of thinking that govern much of your life? What are they and how have you dealt with them? Have you found healing through repentance? How?

---

[1] How to Become a Schizophrenic, John Modrow, Apollyon Press, Everett, Wa., 1995.

[2] Luke 7:47

[3] 1 John 1:9

[4] Psalm 32:3-5

[5] Hope When You're Hurting, Crabb & Allendar, Zondervan Publishing House, Grand Rapids, Michigan, 1996, pg. 26.

[6] Ibid., pg. 27. I don't think Crabb is denying the possible usefulness of the study of child psychology to better understand how certain influences affect development. However, for the sufferer, the connection between explanations

and their present suffering is therapeutically tenuous.

[7] Ibid. pg. 23.

[8] "Deflating Self-Esteem's Role in Societies Ills," Erica Goode, The New York Times, 10/1/02,

[9] Matthew 7:24-27

[10] Matthew 12:45

[11] "Self-esteem May Be Doing Harm," Bernard Bauer, San Jose Mercury News, 2/24/96, front page

[12] Psalm 34:17-18

[13] Psalm 51:5

[14] Psalm 51:6

[15] Proverbs 28:13-14

[16] 1 Peter 2:21

[17] Luke 7:47

[18] Daniel 4:35

CHAPTER 15

Behavioral Therapy and Christianity

> "Then He touched their eyes, saying, 'According to your faith let it be to you.'"
> **Matthew 9:29**

Behaviorism would agree with some of my critiques of more traditional psychotherapies from the previous two chapters. However, they would go much further by denying the therapeutic importance of any insight. They assert that symptomology can be eliminated or mitigated through behavioral programming called "conditioning" or "eradication." Pavlov found that he could make his dog salivate by conditioning the beast to associate the ringing of a bell with food. Once the dog learned that whenever he'd hear a bell, food was forthcoming, he was conditioned to salivate at the mere ringing of the bell. Pavlov learned that certain responses could either be created or eliminated through their association with positive or negative payoffs. Later, B.F. Skinner bragged that he could mold a child into any job profession so desired through the use of positive (rewards) and negative (punishments) reinforcement.

A very common behavioral technique is known as "systematic desensitization." This is often used to desensitize the sufferer from phobias. The sufferer is gradually confronted with the object of their fears. As the sufferer begins to find that they can tolerate increasing doses of the feared stimulus, the dosage is increased. If the client has a fear of flying, for starters, the therapist might confront the client, under relaxed circumstances, with literature about flying. After the client finds that he can tolerate this stimulus, they might then progress to something a little more threatening, perhaps watching movies containing flying scenes. The client might also be encouraged to use the fear to generate poetry, journaling, or storytelling, something that might reorient the fear as a positive instead of the negative that it has been.

Eventually, the client must confront his fears at their most terrifying heights and come to the understanding that, however strongly the phobia is activated, he can handle it. If he hasn't worked therapeutically through his worst nightmares, he'll lack the confidence that he can handle the real thing. A full-blown phobia attack outside of the therapeutic setting might serve to convince him that the therapy was for naught.

This issue is key. Marching through several behavioral scenarios doesn't change neural connections; it doesn't undo the years that terror had deeply etched a neural pathway. Rather, behavioral therapy enables the client to *believe* that he can handle the fear when activated. Each step of systematic desensitization must convince the client, "See, you can take it. It's not going to kill you. You can look it in the face no matter how it rails against you." Patiently confronting the client with ever increasing threats will not achieve anything unless the process convinces him that he can face the challenge. He must come to believe that he is in control whenever phobia bears its fangs.

Once he is confident that he is in control, the fear begins to loose its edge. With each success, he begins to experience a reorientation. The fear becomes domesticated, and it's no longer a threat.

In a new and controversial variation of behaviorism, David H. Barlow subjects his clients to the full extent of their phobias at the outset without any systematic desensitization. For example, a client who feared reading his poetry before others was required to stand up before a hostile crowd of fellow patients staging all forms of threatening behavior.

Barlow is convinced that all of the preliminaries such as relaxation techniques are unnecessary, and he has the statistics to prove it. He reckons his success rate to be "as high as 85%." Slater states that, through Barlow's methods, one client "trained his own brain to *believe* (italics mine) in its strength."

Behaviorism is, in its very essence, belief training. Nothing is accomplished apart from acquiring the belief that the client is stronger than the fear and not visa versa. Slater writes perceptively that "once people disarm their terror, once they *realize* (italics mine) they can survive it, then you have detoxified the problem and in some senses provided a cure." Once they realize that they can survive the terror, they can confidently resume their life without the lurking threat that the phobia will reemerge and again take control.[1]

A CHRISTIAN PERSPECTIVE

Belief is the central element in behaviorism.[2] Clients must come to a belief that they are in control. They must also believe that they can endure whatever the phobia might throw at them. Failing to believe this, they'll continue to dread its reappearance. Reduction of the dread is directly related to their confidence in overcoming it. Furthermore, they have to believe that the lessons they've learned in therapy also apply to their real life. Failing to believe this, there's no gain. They'll still be left feeling defenseless and vulnerable.

The Christian also puts a high priority upon belief. Proverbs claims that as a person thinks, "so is he."[3] Our thinking and believing determine the way we feel, our attitudes, and our behaviors. Our beliefs about a person will determine our attitudes and behaviors toward them. For example, if I believe that my wife is trying to poison me, this will affect the way I feel about her.

However, the Bible is appropriately disparages faith in *self* and self's ability to handle life's challenges. Firstly, there is no compelling reason to believe that the behavioral victory is anything more than temporary. If confidence is based upon the belief that we can endure the threat, it follows that this confidence can be swept away once we experience something unendurable. Slater writes that "his (Barlow's) data suggest that they (clients) stay better up to two years after treatment, beyond which point he has not yet compiled further data."[4] This is a short period. Beliefs change. They're vulnerable to many forms of assault.

Secondly, self is not an adequate object of trust. There are many things that are above our ability. We all must confront death and our gradual undoing by the inexorable aging process. Bertrand Russell, the ardent atheist and mathematician, wrote,

> "Brief and powerless is man's life; on him and all his race the slow, sure doom falls pitiless and dark. Blind to good and evil, reckless of destruction, omnipotent matter roles on its relentless way; for man condemned today to lose his dearest, tomorrow himself to pass through the gate of darkness..."[5]

This portrait places the triumph of the self in its appropriate context. Those traits that we had trusted to keep at bay the fears, threats, rejections, and failures will crumble away. Our appearance, intelligence, and whatever else serves to maintain our performance will begin to vanish despite our best efforts to coax them otherwise. Apart from this, life has its own pains and failures. It's unrealistic to believe that we won't have a major phobic setback. When it happens, the self-confidence will also suffer erosion. It'll be reasonable to conclude that our self-confidence had been ill-founded. We'll understand that we've had placed too much faith in our quickly acquired techniques and beliefs. This is inevitable. Consequently, the Bible likens us to grass that withers and lost sheep who can't survive without their Shepherd.

Thirdly, the ultimate object of our trust must be God. Self can't bear the weight of its own trust. We can't even keep our promises to ourselves. It's hard to be God, especially for us. The success of AA is largely a product of understanding that our lives are out of control, and that we need to relinquish this imaginary control to a

Higher Power. We're not made to carry the burdens and expectations that we place upon ourselves. This reflects the Bible's own understanding. Jesus claims that without Him, we can do nothing. In the same way that a branch must be connected to the vine in order to produce fruit, so we too must be connected to Jesus.[6] This shouldn't argue against human responsibility but against the worry, self-castigation and self-concern which we place upon self. Instead, our lives should be lived in the confidence of God's control and inevitable blessings.

Lastly, there's also the panoramic perspective. What if we succeed in defeating our fears? What have we gained? Jesus warned that it's possible to gain the entire world but to loose what's most important, our very spiritual well being—our relationship with God. Success within the "self-promotion cycle" is deadly. If we succeed in staying at the top of the cycle, it'll just enable us to be arrogant and to look down upon others. Many Christians can thankfully attest that it was due to the love of God that their plans didn't succeed. They fell and had to cry out to One who is truly trustworthy. However, it's inevitable that life at the top of the cycle is only temporary. We'll eventually tumble into the arms of depression from our manic high. "The taller they are, the harder they fall." This isn't to argue that the Christian must remain in their fears. On the contrary, a confidence in God is far more rational and pragmatic than a confidence in self that, by its very nature, is highly vulnerable.

We all need to believe in something. Without the confidence that belief endows, we're left vulnerable to an endless variety of threats. However, which belief or which trust makes the most psychological sense for the long run? Which trust gives us the certainty and confidence when events and feelings are utterly turning against us? It's easy to thrive when events stack up in our favor. At such times, any belief system will do. However, when our self repeatedly fails us, we require a greater Hope, one that's fully available in the midst of our utter failure.

EXERCISE:

1. Have you ever had the experience that you thought you had overcome a problem just to find that it returned later on? What did that do to your confidence? Did you find any resolution to your failure of self-confidence? What?

2. What has your experience with trusting God been like? Contrast this with trusting in self or in something else.

---

[1] "The Cruelest Cure," Lauren Slater, The New York Times Magazine, 11/2/03, pgs. 34-37.

[2] Belief is central to almost all psychotherapies! However, they may differ greatly in their methods to influence belief.

[3] Proverbs 23:7

[4] "The Cruelest Cure."

[5] Entrepreneurs of Life, Os Guinness, Navpress, Colorado Springs, Col., 2001, pg. 38.

[6] John 15:3-5

CHAPTER 16

Cognitive Therapy and Christianity

"For as a man thinks, so is he," **Proverbs 23:7**

You just got fired, and you're feeling angry and depressed. You naturally assume that getting fired *caused* you to become angry and depressed. Not exactly! According to Howard S. Young, a Rational-Emotive Therapy (RET) counselor, it's not that simple. There is a crucial intervening step. To illustrate this, Young uses the example of entering a crowded elevator. You are becoming quite irritated because someone is poking you from behind with a stick. You can't wait for the elevator door to open so you can turn around and give this provocateur a piece of your mind. However, upon turning, you find that the provocateur is a blind man struggling with his walking stick. Immediately your anger disappears! Young concludes that "a change in mind caused a change in feelings."[1]

Your feelings weren't so much the result of the event, but rather of the way you had *conceptualized* the event. Once your thinking was revised, your feelings changed. Based upon this kind of insight, RET and other cognitive therapies have set their sights upon our thought processes. If we can change our thinking, we can also change both our feeling and our acting.

Young then asks, "What kind of ideas cause people to get upset?

Are there some standard ideas that lead to unhappiness?"[2] RET finds that there are specific patterns of irrational, exaggerated thinking reflected in certain statements or words such as "awful" and "terrible" and patterns of unrealistic demands characterized by "must," "ought" and "should."

After identifying irrational thinking and its resulting negative feelings, the RET or cognitive therapist seeks to confront this thinking in order to replace it with rational thinking.

There is much to commend in this perspective. Responsibility is placed where it belongs—upon the sufferer, rather than upon the parents or the society. The important role of thinking and how it causes feeling and acting is made central. However, there are several concerns.

Although feeling often follows thinking, our patterns of thought are often hot-wired into us and are difficult to change.[3] Even with the example of the blind man, the change in thinking (and consequently, the change in feeling) was brought about by *new data*—the sight of the blind man—and not by revised thinking. Consequently, it doesn't follow that whenever we are angered by disrespectful conduct, we can simply invoke the memory of the blind man incident and change our thinking. It's far more difficult to be charitable towards the boss who wrongfully fired you. This requires more than intellectual acrobatics.

We might not have as much leverage in changing our thinking as RET wishes to maintain. By suggesting to their clients that they do have this type of self-control might be setting them up for failure.

A greater problem entails the question of irrational thought. What makes certain thoughts irrational? Is guilt irrational and opposed to sound mental health or is it something we have to listen to for directions? When is anger instructive? Do we act upon it, and in what manner do we act? Which relationships are destructive? Is pain always an evil to be avoided? When must we silently endure it? How do we evaluate whether our course of action was rational? What are the criteria? Is it rational to have an extra-marital affair when our needs go unmet?

Our conception of rationality tends to be myopic. Some things prove successful in the short run but bear poor fruit in the long run. We may feel quite relieved after spilling our gut, but later find that we're paying for it. Is there such a thing as wisdom? How can the therapist know he's wise? Many might find that an extra-marital affair invigorates, but its long term fruitage is deadly, as my sensitivity group leader had discovered. Can we determine the rationality of psychotropic medications if we're unable to determine its long-term effects upon both individual and society? There is such a spectrum of therapies, all contenders for the crown of rationality. Yet there is little agreement.

In addition to these uncertainties, different parties have different pragmatic concerns. What works for the mental institution might not be the same for the client. It might serve the institution to over-medicate their clients. What would rationality demand? There are many different answers depending upon people's interests.

There's another problem. In a recent interview in "Psychology Today," Albert Ellis, the father of RET commented, "If something is irrational, that means it won't work...Rational beliefs bring us closer to getting good results in the real world." From Ellis' perspective, depressed thinking is regarded as negative, self-defeating, and therefore irrational. However, it has been broadly noted that the depressed have more accurate self-assessments than do those people regarded as normal.[4] It should follow from this that "normal" people also should be targeted for cognitive therapy since it's *their* thinking that's more irrational. However, as mentioned before, Shelley Taylor would demure at such a suggestion. According to her, illusions are positive and necessary. With a more accurate self-assessment, we're prone to sink into depression and immobility. It's our inflated self-estimation that keeps us positively involved in living.

Without positive expectations, albeit inflated ones, it's clear that we'll not be proactively involved in the challenges of life. If I don't believe that the store clerk will take my money when I offer it in payment for my groceries, I won't go shopping. If I don't believe that I can make out my check correctly, I wouldn't attempt to make it out at all, especially if there's another way of making my payment. Likewise, if I don't believe that I can teach my students in a way that they can gain any benefit, I won't go to class. Positive expectations are a pre-condition for any activity.

Why do the depressed resist a positive self-estimation and the accompanying positive expectations? After repeated and painful failures, it becomes increasingly difficult to engage life proactively. When amoebae are pricked while actively searching for food, they will contract. After they perceive the threat has passed, they will re-expand to continue their search. If pricked again, they will contract even more severely and stay contracted longer. After a series of pricks, they pathologically contract and stay that way for protracted periods. This eventually invites death.

While walking in the park yesterday, I passed mothers with bright-faced 2-4 year old little girls who smiled broadly to all passers-by. It wasn't surprising to see that the passers-by smiled broadly towards the little charmers. I also passed groups of adults from a program for the developmentally disabled. Their faces and bodies were twisted. They didn't look at anyone, and no one looked at them. Their natures weren't so different from those of the girls. As human beings, we all crave heart-warming human interaction. However, for the developmentally disabled, it is more difficult to obtain this affirmation than it is for the little girls. Who can continue smiling at others when it's seldom reciprocated? After a while we give up, sometimes without realizing that we have given up.

It probably becomes too "painful" for the amoebae to inflate themselves in pursuit of their needs only to be repeatedly pricked. There's a strong element of this in depression. We resist positive thinking because it was this type of optimism that had repeatedly led us into painful defeat and frustration. We cease to believe it. We've loved once; it's too painful to love again.

The depressed need hope; we all need it. Without it, we're not going to extend ourselves out again as much as we might want to.

My therapists had told me that I was a "good person," that I had what was required to be successful. I just had to realize it. Although I couldn't articulate it at the time, I knew otherwise. I knew how hard I had tried, and I knew the painful results of trying and failing. Although I liked what the therapists had been telling me, it was just too hard to *believe* it. They wanted me to trust in myself and my renewed efforts. However, my ubiquitous feelings of failure, shame and inadequacy just wouldn't go away. These feelings spoke louder to my heart than did the therapists' reassurances.

A CHRISTIAN ALTERNATIVE

Life places a lot of pressure upon the self, more than it can bear. Therapy often follows suit by saying, "*You* can do it." While one part of me said, "Yes," another part balked at rebuilding self-hope and its positive expectations for the thousandth time.

We're not made to carry these types of burdens; we can't. We're made for a dependence upon our Creator and Lover. M. Scott Peck writes, "We are guaranteed winners once we simply realize that everything that happens to us has been designed to teach us what we need to know on our journey."[5] We need to know that God is with us every step of the way. Anything less places an intolerable burden upon us and forces us to generate irrational optimism or, as Taylor calls it, "positive illusions."

When our trust is placed upon self, then self has to be inflated to carry that burden, which it can't possibly carry. Life is made of failures and disappointments. If they are often and intense enough, they will necessarily create a negative down-spiral. Who can resist the "amoebae effect?" Then there is the aging process. If the pain and defeats have failed to bring us into step with the reality of our own tenuous existence, aging and impending death won't. These, however, can all serve as "wakeup calls" to inform us that we have to reexamine the perspective of self-trust.

This in itself doesn't argue against Cognitive therapy. There's nothing wrong with scrupulous self-examination to weed out irrational thinking. Self-examination is part of God's mandate.[6] However, we broadly differ in our opinions about what is rational. The Bible teaches that our beliefs about rationality are driven more by what we want than by what is reasonable. It's more a matter of heart than of mind. This is because truth gets in the way of our relentless pursuit after our own agendas.[7]

Aldous Huxley, the author of <u>Brave New World</u> and an atheist, admitted that, "I had motives for not wanting the world to have a meaning; consequently assumed that it had none, and was able without difficulty to find satisfying reasons for this assumption."[8]

This invites a parallel question. Why do "normal" people resort to the irrational thinking of the "shoulds" and "awfuls," and why do they uniformly display distorted self-assessments if living rationally always provides positive results? Where does this irrational thinking come from and why do we engage in it if it causes pain and dysfunction? Perhaps such thinking serves a purpose?

The Christian may find a pattern here. "Shoulds" and "awfuls" tend to magnify the outrage of a trial or an insult. If the offense is *terrible*, then we are *justified* in having our highly exaggerated reaction. If the offense is minor, then we feel ridiculous in trying to get revenge. Why do we tend to want to see ourselves as the innocent victim, and the other as the villain?—because this is the way we feel! When the boss doesn't give us credit for our idea or hard work, it feels like the greatest offense. Why do we feel this way?— because the offense struck at the center of something ultimately important to us. Our self-righteousness or the foundation of our being had been assaulted.

Lacking the Christian worldview, we might recognize the ubiquity of self-righteousness, but fail to see it as a necessary, *substitute* righteousness. We all need to feel valued, and originally we were when we were in perfect union with God. When we rejected God in favor of our own autonomy, we also ignorantly rejected the sense of righteousness or value we enjoyed when in intimate union with God. Lacking this, we had to make do with the fig leaves of our own righteous performance.

If this is the case, trying to change thinking in lieu of being born again is futile. The only way we can effectively challenge our bondage to self-righteous needs and self-justifications is to reclaim our original righteousness. We can then begin to replace the heroin of self-righteousness with the balm of love and forgiveness. Without this, there may be partial and temporary victories, but the overriding need to maintain our self-righteousness will find other justifications once deprived of the now irrational "shoulds."

It all resolves in our Object of trust. If it's great enough, we can face the light of even our own depravity. If the God of the universe is our friend, we no longer need to irrationally inflate ourselves. Failures and rejections may still hurt but these need no longer determine my future; they need no longer contort me. I can smile at the world even if the world doesn't smile back.

EXERCISE:

1. What is your thinking like when you're depressed? Does it affect your self-concept? How?

2. Do you resist thinking good things about yourself when you're depressed? Why?

3. Does it help instead to think good thoughts about God? How?

---

[1] A Rational Counseling Primer, Howard S. Young, Albert Ellis Institute, NY, NY, 1974, pg. 10.

[2] Ibid, pg 19.

[3] This is something that RET readily admits.

[4] This may not pertain to advanced states of depression.

[5] Further Along the Road Less Traveled, M. Scott Peck, Simon & Schuster, NY, NY, 1993, pg. 24.

[6] Psalm 51:6, 1 Corinthians 11:31

[7] Romans 1:18-32

[8] <u>The Journey</u>, Os Guinness, Navpress, Colorado Springs, Col., 2001, pg. 214.

Epilogue

"Therefore let him who thinks he stands take
heed lest he fall." **1 Cor. 10:12**

W hat if we've learned all the principles enunciated in this
book? Would that be enough to shield us from depression
and despair? Let's take it even further. What if we had all wisdom?
Could we then be assured that despair would never darken our
corridors? Banish such a false hope! God would never allow such
self-sufficiency. He loves us too much for that.

Such an expectation is unbiblical. As Paul indicates in the above
verse, thinking that we "have it made" is antagonistic to the
purposes of God. It suggests that if we do come to belief that we're
above certain trials, God will show us otherwise. He won't allow us
to fall captive to the belief in our self-sufficiency.

Paul's strength was his awareness of weakness. He came to see
that on his own he could do nothing.

> "Not that we are adequate in ourselves to consider
> anything as coming from ourselves, but our adequacy is
> from God."[1]

This isn't to say that we haven't gained meaningful wisdom or
self-control. However, without God, we must banish any attitude of
self-sufficiency. Yes, we have learned wisdom, but it's not a
wisdom that enables us to be self-sufficient. Instead, it's a wisdom
that reveals our dependency upon God alone. Mercifully, God will

reveal this to us, although in ways that are sometimes painful.

We like to be able to rely upon ourselves, to be certain that we can get the job done. This is our default mode. When we're unsure that we have what it takes, we experience anxiety. Consequently, we're coerced to rely upon the uncertain will of God. This is less than comfortable. We want to know when and how the job will get done. God doesn't always satisfy us with this type of knowledge. Nor does He immediately rescue us from every painful ordeal.

God sometimes has to remind us that we can't exert the control over our lives that we'd like to have. Even worse, we can't assure ourselves that sin won't get the best of us and that we won't fall headlong into depression. Paul writes that he is unable to do the things he wants to do because of the intense battle of sin within him. This had caused him intense frustration, so much so that he cried out, "O wretched man that I am! Who will deliver me from this body of death?"[2]

Why does God leave us with this intense struggle even after we come to Christ? It's definitely purposeful. He provoked sin to increase by giving the law,[3] but He did this so that we'd see the true status of the sin within us,[4] and in our weakness, continually cry out for His help and receive His loving deliverance.[5]

He does this to safeguard our relationship, which is more precious than anything this world has to offer. God must receive this glory, a glory based upon despair of our self-sufficiency and utter trust in giving God all the glory places our relationship upon a foundation of truth, truth of who He is and who we are.

Any meaningful relationship must be based upon truth. We want to be loved and enjoyed for who we are in truth, not according to what people might erroneously think we are. Should this be any different for God who desires to be worshipped in spirit and in truth?[6]

Our truth is that we are dependent and needy sheep, but we have a God who rejoices in being our Shepherd. This means that we can never in truth give ironclad guarantees that something will get done[7] or that we'll never again be depressed. Only God can give guarantees.

I pray and trust that God won't lead me into temptations that are too great or trials that are too painful, but this is exactly what He does guarantee.

> Many are the afflictions of the righteous, but the Lord delivers him out of them all.[8]

Nevertheless, what He has taught me is inexpressibly valuable. Yes, I still go through trials and wrenching conflict, but I have a safety net, which is tried and true. I know He'll bring me through it. I become depressed, but it doesn't last very long, but long enough to remind me to embrace and to boast in my weaknesses, insults, and infirmities that His grace and strength might come to rest upon me.[9]

I'd rather be free from pain. I give seminars on overcoming depression and despair. On occasion, I hear the voice, "Physician, heal thyself! How can you teach on depression and despair, as if you have answers, when the fact of the matter is that you're still struggling? You're nothing but a hypocrite!" Yet I know that God has brought me so far. He has become a source of joy even in the throes of depression. We'll never be pain-free in this life. It's by His design that He perfects us through our weaknesses.

> "But we have this treasure in earthen vessels, that the excellence of the power may be of God and not of us."[10]

If true love can only thrive when based in truth, then God must continually remind us of the truth of our inability and His ability.

If suffering is our lot, what then is the purpose of this book and the seminars that I give? How does all this teaching serve us? In 1974, I bought a rough-cut hill farm in Appalachia. The house was quite primitive and lacked indoor plumbing. It seemed like the best solution was to gutter the house to funnel the rainwater into a cistern. I later found that the rains were unpredictable and that I'd occasionally have to forego the use of the indoor plumbing.

Wisdom is like the gutters. It awaits the grace from above and channels it appropriately. Without rainfall, the best system of gutters is mere folly and false hope. So too wisdom without the grace from above will prove to be of little profit.

However, wisdom makes room for the grace of God. I soon learned that my cistern was too small. We might get a good soaking rain, but the cistern could only hold so much and the rest of the water would be lost. What the cistern could hold was not enough to see us through the next month of drought. Wisdom not only receives grace by pointing us to the Source, but also enlarges our cistern by excavating the former ruins of thoughts that oppose grace.

In this book I've attempted to impart the wisdom God has rained upon me. As the Law can be reduced to two principles—loving God and loving others—this book can be reduced to one—trust in God alone! I hope I've made it evident that this trust, although very simple, explodes into a vast universe. It involves the nature of God, the Object of our trust, the nature of the trusting agent, and the overwhelming reality that demands our trusting response.

Someday it will be different. Paul reminds us that in this body we "groan,"[11] but there will come a time when the Groom comes for His wife. When this happens, we'll look upon our Groom and see Him as He is, and we'll be totally transformed by what we see.[12]

---

[1] 2 Corinthians 3:5

[2] Romans 7:24

[3] Romans 7:9-11

[4] Romans 7:13

[5] Romans 7:24-25

[6] John 4:24

[7] James 4:13-17

[8] Psalm 34:19, I Corinthians 10:13

[9] 2 Corinthians 12:9-10

[10] 2 Cor. 4:7

[11] Romans 8:23

[12] 1 John 3:2-3

Autobiographical Addendum

I was born at Maimonides Hospital in Brooklyn, June 14, 1947, to second generation Jewish parents. I had one advantage in my search for peace of mind. I knew where I wouldn't find it. My father and his brother had fortuitously graduated from their father's tailor shop to making hand held printers. One thing led to another, and before long, they had a factory and my two younger brothers and I had everything we needed, but this didn't translate into happiness, at least not for me.

I grew up an angry, lonely, and contentious child. My first grade teacher wrote on my report card, "Daniel gets angry whenever he doesn't get what he wants." I don't remember wanting things more than others wanted them. I just thought that my fair share was being withheld, and I was going to do something about it.

Over the next several years, I became very inhibited and probably looked like a well-behaved student, at least superficially. I didn't get along with others and was anything but a team player. I was very willing to get along with them if they would just treat me right, but my idea of 'right' didn't seem to coincide with theirs'. I quit playing basketball at an early age. I was repeatedly accused of 'double dribble.' That meant that they took the ball away from me. I didn't understand that rule and became convinced that I was being unfairly treated. I couldn't allow that to happen, but I found that it was easier to quit playing basketball than to always get into fights.

Around this time, I was kicked out of the Cub Scouts. I was sure that I had been unfairly treated, although I don't remember the circumstances.

Things changed for me at around seventh or eight grade. I had a 'best friend.' We looked alike, enjoyed the same things, and did everything together. We were inseparable. In the ninth grade, we together joined a Jewish fraternity. I had no doubt that this was something that I wanted to do. I was Jewish, and this is where I belonged. For several years, I had experienced a lot of anti-Semitism. The idea of going to school and of facing the pushing and alienation made me cringe. Sometimes I fought back. This was more than the other Jewish youth did. Everyone knew Jews didn't fight back, but I was filled with rage. The rage, however, didn't always enable me to rise to the occasion. Once I failed my best friend when a bully had forced him to leave his seat on the bus. (It's still a painful memory.) We never talked about it. We never talked about any of the anti-Semitic insults we endured. It was just too uncomfortable.

We didn't need to verbalize it. We all knew that a Jewish fraternity was the best thing that could happen to us. We joined without a moment's hesitation. However, reality seldom shakes hands with expectations. On numerous occasions, it seemed to be that my best friend was finding a more enthusiastic welcome from the upper classmen than I. This disturbed me greatly. I no longer felt that he was my best friend. It felt to me that he preferred the company of the upper classmen. This was too much to bear, so I told him to "get out of my life." I did have a plausible rationale for my decision, but I soon forgot what it was. In any case, he was gone.

The following year, my parents approached me with an offer I couldn't refuse. They said that they had noticed that I was depressed and had problems relating to others. "Wouldn't it be nice if you could resolve these issues before you go away to college?" I knew I was going to go to college. That's what Jews did. I never questioned that this would be my lot. The offer sounded good. I wanted to find some peace of mind, some relief from my inner torment. The prospect of finally being free from it was very appealing, and the psychologist was the 'Jewish guru' of choice. However, in 1962, no one bragged about seeing a shrink. There were no other teenagers with whom to compare notes. I was ashamed and knew I'd have to keep it secret, but I agreed to go.

The psychologist was a kindly, elderly, Jewish man. He'd ask me questions about my feelings and relationships and would always start with the same phrase, "What's new on the Rialto?" I didn't know what to expect, nor was I clear about how all of his questions would bring about a cure, but I was sure that there was a connection. It was clear that he wanted to know about my childhood, so I decided to help the process along by trying to recover whatever memories were ready to spring into consciousness. I'd take notes and bring them with me into the session. Gradually, I became convinced that once he'd get a complete picture of my life, he'd pronounce both the diagnosis and the cure, and I'd be free.

Although the psychologist had meant well, I emerged from the process more self-conscious than ever. I had become convinced that I was a product of my environment and that I was so 'sick' that therapy was unable to touch the cause of my misery. I was stripped of any sense of virtue or honor. I also came to understand that I had performed my noblest deeds merely to feel good about myself. In light of this "understanding," life was exclusively about me and my feelings; any concepts of worth were arbitrary creations to impart value and some sense of self importance into silent nothingness where we were nothing more than a cosmic mistake.

I asked my cousin if there was anything 'good' or anything 'bad.' I knew that he would give me an informed answer. He had graduated from college and was already working towards a PhD in anthropology. He was married, so I asked him about love. "Is it anything more than a feeling? Does the feeling stay and what happens if it goes? Do we love because it makes us feel good about ourselves? Then why do we call it 'love'?" He assured me that love changes and deepens with the years, but I was swiftly becoming a nihilist.

By the time that I went away to college in Berkeley, California in 1965, I was convinced that the concepts of 'right' and 'wrong' were mere human creations to give our lives some semblance of order. Although I got involved in a volunteer program directed towards inner city youth at Berkeley, the West Oakland Project, I knew that I was doing it for me, so that I could feel good about myself.

I worked under a compassionate shop teacher who invited me to his home for a Thanksgiving dinner. His guests asked me to explain to them the Berkeley radical uprising.

"It's simple. Students protest because it feels right to them. It gives some sense of meaning and importance to their lives. It also enables them to bond with other like-minded students," I explained. I was surprised they didn't pursue this analysis any further. I felt isolated and alone. Was I too cynical for them?

After my first two months at Berkeley, my parents made some contacts and set up an appointment for me with a psychiatrist that had come highly recommended. It seemed like more of the same, but I was assured that he was highly qualified, and that I could trust him to get the job done.

Meanwhile, I had become acquainted with the writings of nihilist Friedrich Nietzsche, who further convinced me that this was just a 'dog-eat-dog' world, and that it was preferable to be the dog who did the eating. He proclaimed that we were free from moral constraints. They were just arbitrary, the creation of people who wanted to control others. I didn't want to be controlled and could think of some interesting ways to express my newfound independence.

The "Free Sex League" was already in full throttle, and I couldn't find any reason why I shouldn't avail myself of this resource. Although I felt a bit uncomfortable about it, I had to take the plunge. There was nothing wrong with sex; neither was there anything right about it. It was just like eating apple pie, and I liked apple pie. I was just inhibited—a creature socially programmed to be inhibited and modest. But I could do something about my programming. According to Sartre, choice preceded essence. I could choose to create my own reality. This was the only way to live authentically. Besides, sex was supposed to be liberating. As a nihilist, that's where I'd start!

I had heard reports about orgies sponsored by the FSL, and they sounded great to me. That was true freedom! There was no reason why anyone shouldn't fill his plate with what he wanted. Either he was square, which I wasn't any longer, or he was inhibited. The latter was my curse, and I was determined to rid myself of it.

I was getting closer. What would I say when I got there? "Is this where you have the orgy?" That seemed too stiff, too amateurish. The term "orgy" sounded so biological, like a bodily function, like going to the bathroom. But wasn't that why I was there? I wasn't there to find a wife or to have a conversation about Kierkegaard. I was cursed with a mind that was always in overdrive. Was there such a thing as orgy norms? Did you look the women in the face or just play it cool? Should I act excited or just act like this was no different than eating a hamburger? I had never taken an orgy 101 class, so I was at a loss. I had never thought about the dynamics before, nor could I call upon any past precedents to guide my behavior. Would I just throw myself down next to the first naked woman? Was it proper to speak first? Was it considered bad taste to try to strike up a conversation first? That seemed so phony to me. I never liked the idea of eating the main course before the desert. If desert is your thing, then go for it! In the same way, everybody was coming for sex! Conversation would be as artificial as pulling out a deck of cards and asking if anyone played rummy. Besides, I'd feel like a jerk. If I wanted to play games, I might as well join the bridge club.

Upon my arrival, the grounds pleasantly surprised me. I wouldn't have to ask any questions. The door hung wide open into what looked like a Spanish hacienda. A Mexican orange wall enclosed the entire square. Small open living areas were attached to the walls, their windows facing both inside and out. The courtyard was in the center of everything. It was a warm night, slightly balmy. Another uncomfortable thought assailed me. Would I have to take off my clothes at the door? They were all laundered and I had just taken a shower, but I didn't like the idea of nudity. If that were required, I'd have to take the plunge sooner or later. It was understandable that the whole concept of orgy would require that we lay aside our cultural trappings at the door. Besides, the whole concept of façade reeked of the corrupt establishment, and clothing was just another façade. An orgy promised to strip all that away. We had to learn to be ourselves and not hide behind a mask. In what better way could this be accomplished?

Arriving at these foundation stones of truth didn't dispel all of my questions. Would I suddenly strip when someone caught my fancy? That would be awkward and not in keeping with my newfound truths. It seemed to me that we'd more naturally be able to transition into sex with the issue of clothing behind us.

However, as I passed unhindered into the courtyard, I was

suddenly struck by the fact that no one as yet had shed his clothing. Instead, there was a neat row of shoes and socks by the entrance, a relatively painless way to break the ice. There were about 12 guys my own age milling around. It was easy to recognize the host. He was older and seemed to be the only one among us who was relaxed. The rest walked around as if they were in mourning, roaming from one quarter to the next in perfect silence like a cadre of zombies.

"Don't worry fellas," our host reassured us, "the gals will soon be here." A number of us were noticeably comforted. Our host spoke with confidence. He was evidently an old hand at this type of thing. His gray head spoke of many such encounters. His calm countenance proclaimed that he had mastered the uneasiness that many of us were now experiencing. He reclined with a cigarette in one hand, a drink in the other. If we had any questions or fears we needed to confess, this was obviously the guy to turn to. However, there was no such talk. Perhaps the rest were also nihilists, masters of their own fate, stiff upper lip and all that.

An uncomfortable thought suddenly grabbed hold of me. What if I had a gal and some guy tried to ease his way in? Was that what was done at these types of things? This was acceptable at dances. A guy just had to tap you on the shoulder, and you were supposed to make way for him. That was just the way things were done! Were orgies the same thing? I knew that I couldn't do that to another guy. Coitus interruptus! That could cause a fight, but I couldn't envision getting into a fight in my birthday suit. I hadn't heard of any fights erupting at an orgy, but what did I know about orgies?

All these considerations were driving me crazy. I was now supposed to have been free, but the experience of freedom seemed to be eluding me.

The guys continued to mill around impatiently looking at their bare feet. Their reverie was suddenly shattered by the sound of a car parking out front. As casually as they could manage the operation, they peered out through the open door from the inside of the courtyard. A car packed with girls! We looked quickly at one another with nervous delight. "D-Day!" we thought. But as suddenly as the car had arrived, it sped off.

"They probably want to park around the corner." One of the guys was trying to be reassuring. We waited for a moment and resumed the pacing.

"They're coming," our host rang out. Evidently, he knew something we didn't know.

I really wanted to hit a home run tonight, but, at this point, I was content to merely win the ball game. Another uncomfortable thought supplanted the last one. What if the guy went for me? What if I had the girl and a guy just jumped in and began to touch me? Etiquette aside, I knew what I'd have to do. I was a nihilist, not a kink explorer, not a connoisseur of the unusual. I was looking for fulfillment and that type of thing just didn't promise fulfillment. That's where I'd have to draw the line. Everybody drew a line somewhere. If they'd call me "square," then they'd call me "square."

The reverie was again broken by another car parking out front. This time the girls got out of the car and even began moving toward the courtyard door. However, when they saw the sea of hungry male faces, they exchanged a few words and made a hasty return to their car and sped off.

"I don't think we should be standing by the entrance," one of the guys suggested. By now, that had become obvious. We would not be able to tolerate too many additional losses. We were down by ten runs in the ninth inning and our manager tried to rally his team: "Don't worry. It's going to work out fine, fellas!" However, we were no longer finding comfort in his assurances as we had two hours earlier.

Actually, I was beginning to feel a certain sense of relief. Some of the other guys were also breathing more freely. Some even settled onto the ground playing with the grass at their feet.

"I've had enough, man," one exhaled.

" I know what you mean, man," I responded. Several echoed the same sentiments. Our common frustration and perhaps secret relief imparted a common reality, a fleeting bonding. However, several others found their shoes and socks and hastily departed.

"Better odds!" one interjected.

"Yeah," some uttered as we resumed our zombie shuffle. Our host seemed unruffled. More time and cars passed. It was two outs in the last of the ninth. Discomfort gave way to a profound sense of restlessness. Two thoughts crossed my mind. For one thing, I had my studies; for another, we hangers-on were beginning to look utterly pathetic. The ball game was over, and whatever camaraderie we had once shared was melting away into a sense of foolishness.

Our host, sensing the changing mood, called us together. "Well, fellas, it doesn't seem like the girls are coming, but I can provide some oral relief."

That was the sign that several of us were waiting for. Not wanting to offend our gracious host, we began to slowly maneuver towards our shoes and socks in an awkward exercise of nonchalance. It was my only easy decision of the evening.

After this and similar other discouragements, my depression thickened. I was having trouble concentrating on my reading and my relationships were going in the wrong direction. One roommate had gone to the dorm authorities to request a new roommate. One afternoon, I was simply told that I had to pack. Nihilism failed to bring me the freedom I craved— nor would the pursuit of a degree. It was just part of the rat race to outdo the poor 'Joneses.' This wouldn't bring me peace, not in the sixties! However, I was hearing a lot about spiritual answers, getting in touch with spiritual powers.

I've always enjoyed my bicycle. It gave me a taste of freedom. One evening, while pedaling through the Oakland hills, I stumbled across a most incredible graveyard, surrounded by a fitting pearly gate, filled with imposing white mausoleums, like something out of a horror movie. As I progressed up into the hills of the graveyard, I encountered ancient grave markers, wooden markers lying every which way, and streams. It was too good to be true. I was determined to show my extraordinary find to some of my associates, at night of course.

Some others enjoyed the feeling of being 'spooked' as I did. Some couldn't leave soon enough. I invited one fellow philosophy student to sample my find. Ken was thrilled. As we sat together amidst the upper reaches of the graveyard, enjoying the night sounds, he sprang a question on me, "Would you like to have power in your life?" He went on to explain what he meant by 'power.' It sounded like this might be the answer for which I was looking. Instead of feelings and events happening to me, I could be the one who would make it happen. This also meant that I'd have control over my painful feelings. They were getting out of hand. Sometimes all I could do was to take long walks and to listen to Rachmaninoff. His music spoke to me so intimately. It gave me hope that there was something out there, a place of love and completeness. I couldn't define it any better than that, but it comforted me as I tried to fend off frequent thoughts of suicide.

Yes, I wanted the power. Ken came prepared. He slipped me a white stone and a little black book, which I was to read. The stone would accompany me everywhere and remind me of the power. I had many questions, but Ken explained that I'd have to wait for the answers. First, I would have to be initiated and then become part of a secret group. Ken would initiate me himself the following evening.

We met by the entrance to a thick grove of trees on the Berkeley campus. He came prepared with a blindfold and some other paraphernalia. Blindfolded, he led me around over boulders, alongside of trees, reciting what sounded like mumbo-jumbo. Finally, he announced the termination of the initiation. In an air of secrecy, he explained that he'd meet me some time next week after philosophy class, but for now, I was on my own. Meanwhile, I read the book and carried the stone.

"Have you begun to feel differently?"

"No, I read the book and carried the stone, but everything else is still the same," I responded.

Evidently, this wasn't the response Ken was looking for. He asked me to pass him both the stone and the book under the table. I had been rejected, and Ken refused to mutter one additional word.

I was still interested in spiritual things. I had been hearing many stories from reliable people about leaving the body and gaining powers. I was convinced that Ken had no monopoly on power and began to pursue it within other quarters. However, something happened that stopped me dead in my tracks.

It was June, and I was studying for finals in the student building. Fatigued, I placed my head down upon my arms and closed my eyes. When I lifted my head, everything seemed strangely transformed.

Everything seemed so fresh, so new. I decided to leave my studies and walk out into the night. There too everything had been transformed. As I passed people in the night, I'd have to hide my eyes. I loved each one, and for each one, I found myself shedding tears of love incomprehensible to myself. I found that I even loved myself. Every street sign was possessed with a meaning. Each was just where it was supposed to be. I was filled with such a joy as I looked out at everything, as if in a fairyland. And I was bathing in the peace that I had so long sought. Nothing else mattered. However, the next morning it was gone, completely.

Something had happened for which I had no explanation. There was nothing that I had done to bring on this experience. Try as I may, I couldn't bring it back. It came and went, but it left me with some key insights. Everything else paled next to this reality. It was so tender, so beautiful that I knew that everything that I had been seeking seemed ugly in comparison. I lost all interest in finding power. There was nothing coercive about this experience. There were no incantations involved, no way to manipulate its coming. All that I could do was to wait, but I knew that in its own loving, gentle way, this thing or experience (or whatever it was) had the power to totally transform me.

So I waited, but instead of the hoped for transformation, I became even more dissatisfied with my life as it was. I returned to Berkeley the following year and answered an ad for an apartment. I met the realtor but declined the apartment. Before we went our separate ways, he said, "Mann...what type of name is that anyway?"

"I guess it's a German name, but I'm Jewish if that's what you're trying to figure out," I answered.

Without missing a beat, he stated, "That's wonderful. My Lord Jesus is Jewish, and it's the Christian duty to love the Jews."

That was the first time I had ever heard that. These realtors would tell you anything in order to rent an apartment. How shameless! I bit my tongue as he continued about some loving fellowship that he was a part of and how God had a plan for his chosen people, the Jews. He told me about a series of wars that were on the horizon, but that God wouldn't allow Israel to be conquered.

The following year, when I returned to Berkeley, I was again in the market for an apartment. Again, I answered an ad and met the realtor at the apartment. It was the same guy and he had the same exact story. The 'six day war' had just passed. No political event had ever moved me so profoundly. In June, all the Arab nations had arrayed themselves against Israel, determined to thrust her into the sea. Many cut classes that morning to hear the conflicting reports on the TV in the student center. The Arab nations were reporting that they had crushed the Israeli air force and were marching on Tel Aviv. It felt as if it was my life that was being crushed. (I was sure that the other Jewish students all felt the same way.) There was absolute quiet in the TV room as the reports droned on. The announcer passed on a report emanating from Israel, that Israel had crushed the Arab air forces. There were sighs of relief.

"We finally have confirmation," the announcer cried out, "Israel has completely destroyed the combined air forces of Syria, Egypt, and Jordan and is pushing back the invaders on all fronts." This was followed by an uncontrollable, spontaneous outburst from all corners of the room that I can't describe, but one that I'll never forget.

"Yes, you really hit the nail on the head," I told the realtor. This gave him the encouragement he needed to repeat his entire mono- logue. However, this time I knew that this wasn't a speech he had invented to rent an apartment. He was sincere about what he was preaching.

In June 1968, I dropped out of Berkeley for the second time and returned to New York. Finding myself barred from any interesting work, I returned to school, this time to Columbia in January 1969. The peace that I sought continued to elude me. I tried my hand at writing, but found that it was just too laborious. I had become ideal- istic about changing society, but this idealism never took any concrete form. I just took an assortment of courses at Columbia hoping that something would eventually 'click'. I also saw two more psychiatrists, both with disappointing results. Both reinforced my already well established conviction that I was a 'lost cause.'

I finally concluded that the USA wasn't for me. Israel was my destiny. I would find the meaning of life for which I sought in Israel and in fighting for its survival. I sold what I had and bought a one- way ticket to Luxembourg. I would then hitchhike to Israel. It would represent a sort of cleansing process like Moses leading the children of Israel through the wilderness for 40 years. Europe would be my wilderness, albeit for only three months.

My arrival in Israel was contrary to everything that I had expected. I had expected to arrive by boat. I would watch for Israel upon the deck, all night if need be, until I'd sight land. It would be a solitary watch, an experience that I could savor all by myself. Upon reaching Israel, I would fall to the ground, embracing it with my tears. I wouldn't care who saw me at this point.

Reality can be merciless. I couldn't find a boat from Istanbul going to Israel, so I flew. The woman sitting next to me coughed the entire way. We arrived at night without a majestic sunset to herald the fact that I had arrived.

I decided that I wouldn't take the bus along with everyone else to Tel Aviv that night. Instead, I wandered off into the fields by myself, convinced that I alone had the resourcefulness and flexibility to be able to savor such a moment. As I unrolled my sleeping bag to enjoy a contemplative evening under the Israeli stars, I found that I was becoming a feast for the Israeli mosquitoes. The combination of my down bag and the hot Israeli evening proved a lethal combination. The sweat seemed to entice the voracious mosquitoes through the opening of the bag.

The next morning I made it into Tel Aviv. There I was delighted to find that in place of Washington Place or Lincoln Avenue, the streets were named for Theodore Herzl, David Ben-Gurion, and a long line of other Jewish notables. I had come home.

My depression soon found me in my 'promised land'. After spending several days with relatives, I decided to try the Kibbutz, a socialistic community in which the members shared their common tasks, children, and possessions. I settled on one that offered Hebrew classes. However, everyone on my Kibbutz spoke English, something of which I availed myself in favor of learning Hebrew.

Several months later, a Californian named Derick arrived with his Dutch girlfriend Nell. They requested separate dwellings, which I thought odd. They were Christian, and Derick unwisely chose me to proselytize. Although I liked Derick, I would eagerly await him in the dining hall to ridicule his faith; the more people present, the better. I enjoyed talking about spiritual things, but I had a lot of pent up resentment against Christianity, and Derick was my only target. We took several trips together; one was to see his spiritual leader who asked to pray with me. As depressed as I had been, I agreed. After the prayer, he asked if I had sensed anything. In great relief, I answered, "No'.

Derick endured my ridicule for several months. I was preparing to leave the Kibbutz in search of the "ultimate community." Before leaving, I made a drawing for Derick and presented it to him, but he wouldn't take it.

Again, I thrust it at him. "Here Derick, it's for you!" He still didn't take it. "Why don't you want it?"

"I don't want it'" he replied.

"I can see that, but why not?" I asked again.

"You're of the Devil. I don't want anything from you." He was final about it, and I left Kibbutz Ein Dor without seeing Derick again, at least not until 16 years and four children later.

Every Kibbutz was the same story. I was the outsider, a stranger in a strange land, even in Israel. My hopes were beginning to shift from national and social to a spiritual salvation. Whenever I'd meet a person with some kind of faith, I'd ask them questions about it. After Derick, I had managed to put together an impressive string of questions: "How do you know there is a God? How can you really know about this God? How can you be sure that the Bible is accurate? It was written thousands of years ago! How do you know God cares about you with all these other people in the world? How does God influence your life?"

I took my arsenal of questions to a Hasidic Yeshiva with disappointing results, about which I'll comment later. Later, I was on a train going from Nahariya, on the northern coast of Israel, south to Tel Aviv. I stumbled upon an article in the Jerusalem Post about a Californian who received some message from God, and in response, built a boat and brought his entire family to Israel. They had just arrived that day in Haifa. They were mistakenly heading for Lebanon when the Israeli Coast Guard cut them off and led them safely into the Haifa harbor.

I was intrigued by the story and became determined to meet this man. The train was getting ready to pull into the Haifa station at that very moment. I disembarked and made my way to the harbor where they were being held. They had entered Israel illegally without a visa and had to await judgment from the Israeli government. Since Israel wasn't in the market for any more Christian missionaries, permission didn't seem likely.

I was allowed to enter into the harbor enclave but was told that the Harrisons. (I'm not sure if that's their name.) were being held in the Coast Guard area, which was off-limits to civilians. I found the Stationmaster of the harbor and asked if he could arrange entrance for me into the Coast Guard area to see the Harrisons. He asked me why I wanted to see them, and I explained that I had read the article in the paper and wanted to see them.

He pushed the right button, and Harrison met at the gate. He escorted me onto his boat where we talked for the next several hours. I immediately hit him with my barrage of questions, and he uniformly responded back with Bible verses.

"Don't quote verses to me. First you have to establish that it's the Word of God. Only then can you use it as part of your proof." However, he just continued to quote his verses. Meanwhile, I thought to myself, "Is this why I got off the train? Why didn't I realize that this is what I'd get and nothing more?"

I looked at the tattoos running up and down his arms. Clearly, he had had a wild youth and now had to resort to religion to comfort his guilty conscience. His religion was no more than a sociological phenomenon from what I could tell, something that had no relevance to me. It was getting dark. His wife and five children who had been wandering the dock, returned to the boat where she descended to the kitchen to prepare their evening meal. It was time for me to leave. Harrison had been very gracious in talking to me, but I had drawn a blank. I got up to excuse myself when he hit me with the long overdue request.

"Can I pray with you?" he asked. I couldn't refuse him after all his graciousness. He also requested my address in Israel, which I gave him, but never heard from him again. I emerged from the harbor area into the Haifa night air. I walked along the commercial streets surrounding the harbor. Suddenly I realized that everything had changed as they had four years earlier. They still had the same shape, but they were now strangely transformed. Again, I had to hide my tear filled eyes from perfect strangers. I wandered around marveling at everything for its glow and freshness. My problems were once again far behind me, even non-existent. I couldn't even imagine my depression and self-loathing. An unstoppable flood of light, love, joy, and peace washed them away. Where did it all come from? It was now 1970, four years after my first encounter in 1966. What brought it on? I didn't know. Maybe I had caught some of Harrison's unmistakable enthusiasm? I was convinced that it represented some form of psychological acrobatics. If I could just learn the trick, my life would always be surrounded by joy.

I don't remember where I spent the night, but by the morning, whatever it was was gone, and every acrobatic twist and turn utterly failed to coax it back. I was left as perplexed as I had been the first time.

I subsequently relocated to a Kibbutz north of the Sea of Galilee where I married a petite French woman who was working there as a summer volunteer. We were making arrangements to become members of a Kibbutz on the Lebanese border. However, there were some hard feelings, and we decided to leave. Françoise no longer wanted to remain in Israel; nor did she want to return to France. So we returned to the USA. By now, we had both become misanthropes and wanted nothing more than to live apart from the rest of the human race. We reckoned that the best way to accomplish this was through subsistence farming. We'd raise everything that we needed and live as basically as we could. To achieve this goal, we found a farm in rural Appalachia at the end of a dead-end dirt road.

Nature was at peace with itself. If we could live in harmony with nature, we would become one with nature's peace. Besides, life would be fulfilling once we learned to depend upon ourselves for our daily needs, living in a way that doesn't 'rip-off' nature. Consistent with our philosophy, I didn't want to use any chemical fertilizers or polluting engines. We'd have to find an animal to plow our soil and haul our wood. This might not be the road to happiness and gaiety but certainly to peace and harmony.

One day, our neighbor Johnny called to inform me that he knew of a mule I could work. I was all ears. I picked up Johnny, and we drove to Old Man Coulter's. No one else was called 'Old Man' so and so. I surmised that Coulter was referred to this way for reasons that went beyond the mere fact of his age, but I didn't know why and had never asked Johnny about this. Johnny seemed to know everyone in these hills. He had been here for a long time, and, as was the case with other farmers, he had done a lot of trading. Few could afford new equipment. It generally had to filter down to most of us through a long series of unknown hands. We had to be resourceful. Johnny was good with his hands. He could fix anything. In these hills, it was a matter of survival. He also knew his animals, even their personalities, and had a story to tell about each of them. That's why I was eager to have his recommendation on a work animal.

When we pulled up, Old Man Coulter was in his barn. Johnny gave a holler, and he emerged wiggling from side to side with a giant grin masking his furrowed face and his hunger for the deal. I knew it would take 15-20 minutes before we could begin talking about his mule. That was the price of doing business in the hills. It was an art that had to be performed with tact. Besides, I didn't want to seem too excited about his mule. It might influence the price.

Finally, Old Man Coulter got the mule out of the barn, harnessed him up, and attached his plow.

"He sure can plow," Johnny yelled out. Indeed, without jerking or moving from side to side, the powerful beast was plowing out deep straight furrows. Johnny was noticeably impressed. I paid Old Man Coulter his asking price of $200, and we loaded the mule up into my pickup. I dropped Johnny off at his farm and proceeded home, anxious to do my plowing before the heavy spring rains. This was a big step towards self-sufficiency. Additionally, I welcomed the manure that the mule would produce. It all fit together, and peace was in sight.

As soon as we got back to my place, I harnessed the mule up, placed the bridle in his mouth, and attached my newly obtained plow. We were ready to go! Standing behind the mule with the bridle reigns in my hand, I repeated the word I had heard Old Man Coulter utter with indisputable results. "Hee-haw!" However, this time, there was one difference. The mule failed to move.

"Hee-haw!" I yelled louder, snapping the reigns. Perhaps the mule didn't understand my New York accent. I therefore, repeated my command as I pushed him forward from behind, again to no avail. I repeated the procedure leaning heavily against the mule's rear. He didn't flinch.

By now, I was becoming frustrated with my costly purchase. I scrutinized his imperturbable countenance as I contemplated my next move. Perhaps there was a communication gap. Standing in front of the mule I began pulling his bridle in my direction. I was sure that this would communicate that I wanted him to move forward. However, he ignored my latest strategy as he had all the others.

After attempting several other manipulations with equal success, I threw down the bridle and raced to the phone. This mongrel creature had become my burden because of Johnny's recommendation. He could at least get the mule to move! I was hoping that Johnny wouldn't be out in the field. After spending $200, I was eager to obtain some reassurance that I hadn't purchased the booby prize of the century. If he didn't answer his phone, I'd just have to go find him.

Fortunately, he was still in his house and patiently listened as I rambled on about my disappointment.

"I'll be right down, Danny," he replied in his country drawl. "You just have to show the mule that you know more than he knows."

I plowed over in my mind this unlikely piece of country wisdom until Johnny arrived. Once he did arrive, he reiterated the same perplexing message in a slower drawl than usual so that I wouldn't miss the point.

"The mule thinks he knows more than you know. You got to show him that you know more than he knows," Johnny added. I was annoyed with Johnny's display of omniscience, but I was in no position to protest. How could he know what the mule thought and that the mule would be amenable to recognizing the superiority of my knowledge once he'd see such a display?

The mule remained immobile at the side of the barn where I had tied him up.

"How would I teach him that I know more than he knows?" I disguised my annoyance at Johnny's presumption with a show of confusion.

"I'll show you how," Johnny casually answered. He then picked up a five-foot length of two-by-four, which was lying against the barn. Before I could protest, Johnny wound up the two-by-four as if it were a baseball bat and smacked a home run right across the mule's face.

"Now he understands," Johnny confidently announced. I was incredulous. I had just spent $200 for that mule which Johnny had almost killed, but before I could collect my thoughts to lodge a complaint, Johnny and the mule were plowing my garden with an ease that both astounded and gladdened me.

"You see, Danny. He thinks he knows more than you. You got to show him he don't." It did seem like the mule had gotten the point. After such a blow, I was sure that the magnitude of the lesson would exercise a salutary effect upon my own relationship with the animal even after Johnny had taken his leave. I was impressed by Johnny's finesse, but to him, this was all part of the daily life of a farmer, nothing to be proud about. He suddenly jumped into his vehicle explaining that he had to return to his farm leaving me holding the bridle.

Meanwhile, the mule was seemingly obediently waiting for me in the garden where Johnny had left him. I admired the plowed furrows. To a farmer, what was expeditious was also beautiful. The ministrations of the plow had rolled the crumbly brown earth over in neat furrows. It was a thing of beauty, and it was *my* earth. I had applied layers of manure and observed that I had been richly rewarded by the copious presence of earthworms scrambling for lower ground away from the predatory birds. Very pleased with myself, I ran my hand through the crumbly soil. This would produce a great garden! Grabbing the bridle, I resumed my position to the rear of the mule.

"Yahoo," I commanded without a corresponding response. I felt my heart sink. Yanking the bridle reigns, I repeated my command, again without any response. This had now become a personal affront.

"You worked for Johnny and you worked for Old Man Coulter.

Don't tell me you're not going to work for me!" I was furious. I would not allow this to happen. Standing in front of the mule, I screamed a barrage of the most caustic insults that I had accumulated over the years into his stoic face. I then resumed my place behind the mule, hoping that this verbal assault would give him sufficient reason to believe that I meant business. He remained unconvinced.

I knew what I had to do. I ran to the barn and retrieved the two-by-four and stroked the side of the beast's face with it. I was sure he got the point. The blow to his face that he had sustained would still be fresh in his mind. He would only require a reminder. Dropping the plank, I ran to the mule's rear to pick up the reigns before he'd forget the lesson. I screamed my orders and waited for the response. The mule remained unperturbed.

Feverishly, I ran to his front grabbing the two-by-four in both hands. Jumping back and forth, I swung it around like a windmill as I emitted what I had hoped would sound like blood-curdling yells. I swung it around the mule's head multiple times without contacting him. The mule seemed to be oblivious to my maneuvers as if he had seen this type of thing from frustrated hippies many times before. This wasn't encouraging; nor did I find any reason for encouragement once I again took the reigns.

I knew what I'd have to do. The mule was calling my bluff, and I'd have to raise the stakes. I was not about to lose my original investment. The mule wore a look that seemed to say that he was bored by the whole proceeding. I would have to show him that there was an antidote for his boredom and that I was willing to use it.

With the two-by-four in my hands, I wound up as far as I could go. The mule's impassive expression filled me with fury. I had every right to deprive him of it. He was mine. I had bought him to do a job, a job that he had failed to perform. I had already called upon Johnny once. I knew what he would say: "You have to show the mule that you know more than he knows!" But I had showed him that already, in every way possible. How else could I warn him? If I had to beat him, it was his fault. The mule was making me do it to him.

I dropped the two-by-four. I couldn't do it. What could I do with this mule now? Perhaps he did know more than me, but I couldn't provide him room and board for the rest of his life. That would be too costly. Besides, I wouldn't want the reminder of my failure looking me in the eyes every morning as he ate my hay without recompense; nor could I bear seeing his bored face mocking my incompetence.

I discovered that Old Man Coulter had made a sizeable profit from our transaction, and that he hadn't the slightest interest in buying the mule back; nor were there any other unsuspecting hippies in the area who might have been interested in owning my relic.

I was blandly informed that I had only one recourse; one to which I reluctantly resorted. The truck from the feed company arrived promptly the next day. They had no problem loading the mule onto their truck. Evidently, they knew more than the mule knew, but this didn't comfort me.

Finally, I broke down and bought an old tractor and a chain saw. Yes, it was a compromise, but the natural life hadn't been panning out. Rather than paying dividends of peace, I was reaping worry and heartache. I enjoyed raising a garden and heating with wood, but I found that this wasn't the simple life many had promised it would be.

About this time, the Jehovah Witnesses discovered me. Their visits were welcome, and I found that I had a renewed interest in spiritual things. However, I felt it imperative to advise the Witness, that although I enjoyed his visits, I was Jewish and didn't have any intention of converting. He seemed OK with that.

The last time the Witness came, he was accompanied with a carload of Witnesses. I made tea and we sat down to talk. It soon became apparent that they had come for the kill. They wanted to know what objections I had.

"I'm not convinced about a lot of things," I retorted.

"You're trusting too much in your mind. You have to let go of that," they responded.

"Why then are you trying to appeal to my mind?" Shortly afterwards, they departed but left me with a book critiquing the theory of evolution. I read it to find that this theory wasn't as sound as I had once thought.

When I returned to New Jersey to visit my parents, they

suggested that I go see Rabbi Morris (false name) with my questions. I met with him at his office. He pointed to the electric socket and informed me, "Judaism is like that socket. There's power there. You just have to learn how to plug in."

I liked the analogy. It made spirituality sound very simple and straightforward. The Rabbi gave me a stack of books, and assured me that these would enable me to plug in. I had my doubts, but he seemed very confident about it. He also invited me to respond to him by cassette tape if I had any questions. I told him I would, but I had never done this before and was afraid that I'd feel awkward trying.

I read most of the books, but they sowed more questions than answers. Nevertheless, I sent lengthy letters off to two of the authors laying out my life and struggles and asking them how God might be an answer to these concerns. I never heard back. Subsequently, I heard that Rabbi Morris had run off with his secretary leaving his synagogue to another. He was having his own problems plugging in.

My wife and I were also becoming more estranged. We went to a therapist together, but the therapy wasn't doing us any good. One day, while my wife was away from the farm, I began to work on the chain saw. The oiler had become gummed up. Due to my effort to save money, I had been using used motor oil instead of the clean oil. I was now trying to run kerosene through the oiler mechanism in order to clean it out. Carelessly, I allowed the tip of the saw to engage a hard surface of a tree. I was totally unprepared for what happened next. With the saw being gunned, the chain saw bucked back at me and slammed into my forehead. Terrified, I lifted my hands to my forehand to ascertain what of my skull I had left intact, if anything.

As I lifted my hands up, I saw that my left hand was hanging half off, and the blood was squirting out as if someone turned on the spigot. I fled to the house with my hand pinned to my side in hope of stemming some of the bleeding. I grabbed the wall phone in the kitchen and dialed the operator. In 1976, '911' wasn't even a dream. The operator didn't answer, so I dialed the one number I knew, that of a neighbor living within two miles of my farm. This was my last resort, so I let the phone ring 16 times. Meanwhile, I said a prayer that Jews say before they die.

"Here, O Israel, the Lord our God, the Lord is One. And you shall love the Lord..." The phone rang about 18 times until it was answered.

"Come quickly, I'm bleeding to death," I cried as our neighbor's son answered the phone. Anita, my wife, and I discovered, when we visited my rescuers two years ago, that they were getting into their car to leave for town as they heard the phone ring. As the son was getting into the car, his father said, "Don't get the phone. We have to get into town already."

The son fired back, "Dad, what if it's someone hurt who needs our help?" With that he ran back to get the phone.

After the call, I settled back into the pool of blood, which had accumulated at my feet. Suddenly, I knew that I wasn't going to die. There was Somebody there who wasn't going to let that happen. I was filled with a burst of joy and peace that drove away all the clouds of doom. I felt totally protected. I knew that the Divine was present, and He loved me. Even if I did die, it wasn't important because I knew that I'd be with Him.

The joy was so intense that I lifted my one good arm and cried out, "I'd gladly give You both arms and both legs just to have You." The God who had been wooing me for years had finally revealed Himself. I had seen His glory on two prior occasions but didn't know it was Him. For some reason, He had allowed me to continue in my blindness without realizing His presence. Now, at His designated moment, He made His presence known.

In utter joy, I was laughing out loud amidst the blood. Nothing could silence my laughter, and I continued to laugh as the Lamphiers drove up, heard the chain saw still running, and burst into the kitchen prepared to see the worst. They later described it as a "murder scene" with blood pasted all over the walls.

Jean had been a nurse, and she tied up my wounds after calling for the medical squad. She and her husband Dale later said that they had never seen anyone so close to death. I was changing colors. Although I don't remember it, they said that I had been drifting in and out of consciousness.

I still didn't know who God was, but I knew that He was so glorious, so full of love, that He overshadowed any of my ethnic loyalties. I had been searching for God but wanted Him my way. He had to meet my specifications. For one thing, He had to be a Jewish God and not a Christian One. For another thing, I wanted intellectual certainty and not a cotton candy faith. But He had already answered this latter concern through His undeniable, sustaining presence.

I convalesced four days in the hospital. My parents raced out to visit me from New Jersey and were surprised to find that I was in such good spirits. They understood that something miraculous had taken place but were afraid to ask about it. Meanwhile, the Lamphiers brought me some Christian books to read. They spoke about a God who loved us and died for us. The first part was certainly agreeable, but the second part was a bitter pill. I still had a great problem with the idea of Jesus Christ. Many Jews had died in his name, and many who hated Jews called themselves Christian. Besides, the idea of someone dying on the Cross for me was difficult to believe, and I had difficulty seeing myself as a sinner. If I had done wrong, it wasn't me who had done the wrong but my psychological conditioning. If I didn't have this conditioning, I was sure that I wouldn't do wrong. Furthermore, the idea of the Cross seemed utterly absurd. How was it that God couldn't love me before the crucifixion, but that afterwards, everything was fine? How could I believe that? Did I want to believe that? It seemed like a bunch of "hocus-pocus."

By the time I returned home, the peace that I had been experiencing was about to disappear. I couldn't bear the idea of returning to the same old thing, so I prayed fervently to God, "God, I don't care who You are. I just want to know You as You truly are and won't leave any stone unturned until I find You."

There was one stone I had purposely left unturned. That stone was called Christianity. To me, becoming a Christian had always meant "selling out" or "joining the enemy" or simply becoming brain dead. When I was about 14, there was talk that a certain Jewish family had converted to Christianity. I was filled with disgust at the thought of it. How could Jews do such a thing? We all thought it a 'cop-out.' They wanted to deny their Jewishness and join the dominant culture for personal gain. We understood that if the Gentiles couldn't kill us, they'd at least try to convert us, anything to prevent us from remaining Jewish. However, after what I now knew of God, these concerns no longer carried the weight they once had.

I prayed, "God, if Jesus is the Savior and Messiah that the Hebrew prophets wrote about, You're going to have to show me." I needed to go to the hospital to see my surgeon for the first weekly exam. I only had one vehicle, a stick-shift truck, which I could no longer drive. I had to hitch my way to the hospital. I prayed, "Lord, if this is true about Jesus Christ, I pray that You'd confirm it by granting me some good rides to the hospital."

My first ride came promptly. A redneck-type with half his teeth missing waved me into his vehicle. I was a little reluctant to enter seeing two other toothless men in the car. This didn't look like a God-given hitch, but far out in the 'sticks,' without many other vehicles navigating these roads, I couldn't refuse it.

"Where ya goin, partner?" he asked.

"Holzer Medical Center. I need to see my surgeon about this chainsaw injury."

"Nasty things, chainsaws." I waited for him to tell me how far he was going, but he didn't do so. Instead, I'd wait to see what God would do with this ride. He took a turn onto the highway that would bring us to the hospital and gunned the car.

"Just want to see if she can still do it." He accelerated his car past the speed limit. Since he was heading straight for the hospital, I didn't want to criticize him for his driving. Suddenly, the front tire blew out. Miraculously, the car held the road.

"We'll get ya ta Holzer, partner." With a flat tire, my crew dropped me off at the front entrance of Holzer. I couldn't have asked more from a limousine.

On the way back, a single, corporately-attired man stopped at the beckoning motion of my thumb. He rolled his window down and apologetically informed me that he doesn't stop for hitchhikers, but to his embarrassment, couldn't determine why he stopped for me.

"You might as well get in," he finally motioned, breaking the awkward stalemate.

I returned home jubilant, but that only lasted until the next day, when I again assessed the entire story of a Messiah and a Cross as highly unlikely. However, that was an assessment that cast me back into my pre-encounter malaise. I would have to do some more exploring before I could take such a radical leap.

The books that the Lamphiers had brought me while I was convalescing talked about people getting together for prayer and Bible study. It also talked about how Jesus Christ worked through them as a group, and how He answered their prayers. This would be my next step. I'd find a prayer group. Actually going to church was more than I was ready to deal with. For me it represented a rejection of everything with which I had once identified— family, history, and culture. It also represented joining the enemy, an enemy who hated me. How could such an institution be the caretaker of the truth? Where was the evidence? However, individual Christians might be more approachable.

I began to make inquiries about prayer meetings. Even in Appalachia, few could tell me where I could find one. One evening, an elderly woman called and gave me the info. I asked a neighbor to drive me into Gallipolis one evening, and there I was. I entered a room set apart from the church, reassuring myself the whole time that I wasn't really entering a church.

There was only one elderly woman there. About twenty chairs were arranged in a circle, and I found myself one and lowered my bandaged head. I was a sight! My arm was also bandaged and in a sling. The room began to fill. I noticed that as the people entered, their attention was drawn to my conspicuous appearance. They then would try to casually look to others, hoping there might be someone there who could make an introduction.

Finally, one woman sat next to me and introduced herself. In response, I gave her my name but nothing further. After conversing with several others, she turned back to me.

"Have you ever been here before," she asked as friendly as she could.

"No." I gave her little opportunity to pursue the conversation further.

After a minute, she turned back to me, "Do you know Jesus Christ as your Lord and Savior?"

"Look lady," I responded, intending no malice, "don't worry about me. I didn't come here to draw a lot of attention to myself. You just do what you got to do. When you sing, I'll sing. When you pray, I'll pray."

With that, the meeting started. They stood and sang three hymns that three people had requested. If this music was intended to get people into a spiritual mode, I could think of a lot more inspiring music.

Then they sat down and took turns throwing things out that they wanted the others to pray for. After they were finished with their requests, we stood, held hands, and lowered our heads, as people took turns praying.

I felt very uncomfortable holding hands and standing in a circle. I lifted my head and surveyed the people. These weren't people that I would choose as friends. They were different. Their ideas and attitudes were different. They even looked strange to me.

While I was surveying this strange scene, I saw others clandestinely lifting their heads to survey me. When they saw me eyeball them, they'd quickly drop their heads as the prayer meeting continued. However, I was surprised that there was one couple out of the group to whom I was drawn.

After the meeting was over, several people came up to me to tell me that they hoped I'd return. Among my greeters was the couple. I don't remember their names, but I'll call them the Dawsons.

"We'd love for you to come over to our house. We have a Bible study which meets there, and it would make us happy if you'd join us." I took their address and told them not to expect me, all the time knowing that I'd come.

I felt more comfortable at their home than at the prayer meeting. They made me feel wanted, so I continued to return. I'd ask my many questions and inject my many doubts. Although I often didn't get satisfactory answers and probably made them feel a bit uncomfortable, they continued to welcome me until they moved to the big city, Columbus, Ohio.

I was making baby steps, which eventually took me to church. The pastor seemed to have his act together. He could answer my question without missing a beat, although I still wasn't convinced by his answers. However, I began to study the Bible and discovered that Jesus had fulfilled many of the Old Testament prophecies. I also learned about how He was the ultimate sacrifice, fulfilling all the requirements of the Mosaic Law. In light of this, I began to see that the New Testament wasn't something that had been arbitrarily tacked onto Hebrew Scriptures by people who hated Jews. I was surprised to find that Jews had written it, and that Jesus Himself was a Jew. I was shocked. The barriers were coming down.

My biggest problem was the fact that I was still me. I continued to struggle with depression and doubt. I had expected that I would always experience Christ as I had in my "pool of blood encounter." It seemed like I was where I was supposed to be, but it didn't resemble what I had expected. I thought that I'd no longer suffer, that I would become self-sufficient, and that depression and self-consciousness would become a thing of the past. It had seemed reasonable to me that once I had opened the right door to the truth, I would always be able to live in "encounter" mode. Something must be wrong!

Perhaps I needed to be baptized? I went to a pastor who explained to me the rationale for baptism. Although his explanation didn't coincide with my heightened expectation of instant transformation, I went through with the baptism.

However, I was growing in the understanding of Hebrew Scriptures and began to see how the Cross had been anticipated by Moses and the Prophets. It was the Messiah who would make the ultimate sacrifice to fulfill all the offerings of the Temple. Isaiah's prophecies were particularly impressive.

> Surely He has borne our griefs and carried our sorrows; yet we esteemed Him stricken, smitten by God, and afflicted. But He was wounded for our transgressions, He was bruised for our iniquities; the chastisement for our peace was upon Him, and by His stripes we are healed. All we like sheep have gone astray; we have turned, every one, to his own way; and the Lord has laid on Him the iniquity of us all" (Isaiah 53:4-6).

My chainsaw injury had eliminated farming as an option. School began to loom attractive to me. I had always wanted to help people, but I had felt that I lacked the resources. Now, I was beginning to feel confident that I had them.

In January 1977, I enrolled at Ohio University in Athens, Ohio to complete my undergraduate degree. I was thrilled to find out that I could complete it in a mere 1½ years. Although it didn't go smoothly, I found that I was a much more successful student than I ever had been and gave thanks to my newfound faith. I was following God's commands, and I was beginning to reap some of the payoffs.

I performed my Social Work fieldwork at a community mental health center. With one exception, I enjoyed the weekly meetings where the clinicians conferenced their cases. Even though they were well aware of my faith, they made no effort to disguise their contempt for their clients' Christian faith.

I bit my tongue. I didn't know what to say and was sure that anything that I might have said would have been regarded as an inappropriate expression of my own insecurities. In lieu of a tirade, I resolved that someday, I would start a Christian counseling agency where people of my faith wouldn't have to subject themselves to disguised contempt, albeit hidden. A year later my resolve began to take form. I sent letters out to all the local clergy, followed them up with a personal visit, and set up my fledgling office with a big leather reclining chair

Through all of this effort, I only got one client. However, I placed such burdens upon his back that he literally fled my office to never return. However, I didn't take this as an indication that perhaps my approach might be faulty. I was convinced that the application of the same principles that had seemed to work for me would also work for others. However, all of this was called into question by the events of the next few years.

Around that time, I endured several setbacks. At the time, they didn't seem like great setbacks. I was living midweek in Athens with some friends and working at the Adult Parole Authority. My wife called me while we were engaged in Monopoly. She informed me that she wouldn't be moving up to Athens, to the house we had already selected, but would be leaving me in favor of a mutual friend.

I returned to the monopoly board. "Whose move?" I asked. I wasn't overly perturbed. The marriage had been painful, and finally the pain would be gone—at least that's what I thought.

I was now a free man with two households to maintain. I found a rented room and continued working as a parole officer until my layoff. Meanwhile, I made some new friends: two couples who saw themselves as a radical Christian community. Although I cherished my independence and didn't share their radical views regarding community, we all became close friends. The group would cook meals together, and I was always welcome. They enjoyed talking about feelings and political/philosophical ideas, and I fell right in with them, even though we didn't always agree. Nevertheless, they were idealistic about life and living 'on the edge' for our Lord, and so was I. I didn't suspect that they had any designs upon me apart from the simple enjoyment of our friendship.

One evening, while lounging around their house, I stumbled upon a single page paper entitled "Manifesto." I was shocked by what I read! It was clearly their "manifesto." It had their names on it. Among other things, the 'manifesto' contended that those who weren't living in Christian community were in direct rebellion against the Lord, living outside the parameters of His grace. Instead of living in love under the authority of a Christian community, such people were living autonomously and selfishly.

I was stricken. This seemed to pertain to me. I was living apart from submission to a community, making my own decisions. But what of the friendship that we had shared, the mutual respect and acceptance that had been extended? Had I been mistaken about all the sincerity of their friendship? Did they regard me as a rebel against the Lord as their "manifesto" seemed to suggest I was? I had to iron this matter out with them.

They were very unapologetic about their "manifesto." This wasn't what I hoped for. Perhaps they regarded certain people as exceptions to their specified principles? No, there were no exceptions. I was clearly in rebellion. I had refused to submit to the demands of Christian community and had determined to live my own individualistic, selfish lifestyle where I had my own bank account and autonomy.

How could I have been so wrong about four people whom I had come to consider as my best friends? Despite our obvious differences, they had impacted my life, and I had thought that I had impacted theirs. I had begun to appreciate their point of view, and I had thought they had mine. No, it was all a gross delusion. Subsequently, we began to drift apart.

Several weeks later, I awoke at my rented room on E. State St. with a feeling of dread. I neither drank nor smoked, but I felt a powerful urge for oral stimulation to quell the anxiety that had begun to well up within me. I got into my car and drove to the `supermarket, which was open at 7:00 AM. I hastily stuffed a sandwich down my throat and began to drive back to my room. The dread grew into panic, and I began to pass out. I quickly pulled my car over to the side of the road, got out, and started to run. I didn't know what else to do. I was more terrified than if a lion was pursuing me. I had had a couple of near-death encounters. Yes, they were terrifying, but nothing compared to what I was now experiencing.

I ran and ran. It didn't matter how much my chest and sides hurt. The terror overshadowed everything else. After an hour or so, I stopped to survey the internal landscape. Was the terror still there? It didn't seem to be. I transported myself back home where I could further review the damage. The terror seemed to have left as mysteriously as it had come. I was shaken, but I had been able to handle it by running. If it returned again, I'd do the same thing.

I had recently enrolled in a graduate program in "guidance and counseling." I would sit in back of the room. If the terror returned, I knew what I'd have to do. It did return—many times! I was no longer able to outrun it. It caught me at the most vulnerable moments, at moments when it was least welcome. I knew that something was radically the matter with me. How could I have been so presumptuous as to want to counsel others when I was an absolute "basket case?" Shame covered me to the point of asphyxiation.

I no longer could tell when a panic attack started and when it ended. I was always in dread. The attacks rendered me dysfunctional.

I did somehow limp through my courses until the end of the quarter. It was unthinkable to go on.

I didn't know who to talk to. Who could understand such a thing? I couldn't begin to understand it myself. I had developed such a great disdain for the secular counseling community, that death was far more preferable than degrading myself further by seeking their help. Furthermore, there were no Christian counselors within hours of me and besides, what could they tell me? I had reassured myself that I had been living the Christian life the way I was supposed to, and look what happened to me! How could this have happened? I could generate only two hypotheses: either the Christian religion was a miserable sham or God had rejected me, perhaps for my sub-standard Christian performance?

I usually gravitated to the second hypothesis. My early convictions had again been confirmed. I was a loser. Perhaps I was still too damaged by my past? Perhaps I didn't have enough faith or perhaps there was something else that was so utterly distasteful about me that God kept me "at hands length," if He kept me at all?

For many, Christianity seemed to be working admirably. They had had their prayers answered, and they were far more joyful than they had been. This was no longer the case for me. What had been the bedrock of my faith was now taken away. My prayers weren't answered, and I was anything but happy. Life had become a nightmare, and I was the prey in some horror movie, one that never came to an end.

Terror, self-contempt, and depression were my constant companions. The things I used to do I could no longer do. The people with whom I used to relate, I had to now avoid. Having a casual conversation had become something beyond my ability. I felt so ashamed of myself that I couldn't allow anyone else to see me. Surely, they'd see me in the same light in which I saw myself. I was worse than the slime on the inside of the toilet bowl and couldn't bear the idea of others seeing this piece of slime.

I would take my walks in the darkness and cry out into the night. Yes, I still cried out to God. I had nowhere else to cry. Perhaps He'd see my pain and brokenness and take pity upon me? In any event, I wasn't getting a response. Was He a sadist taking pleasure in a freak show? How could He possibly love me? I could think of many reasons why He wouldn't!

I needed to talk to someone but who? I returned to the two couples. It didn't surprise me that they had a ready explanation for my demise. Mercifully, God was showing me that I was in a state of rebellion against Him and that these panic attacks were overtaking me to prove it. All I had to do was join them, and the reason for these trials would be entirely removed.

Perhaps they were right. I turned over half of my money to them and moved in the following day. They felt it only fair that I wouldn't have to give them all of my money until the end of the trial period. Along with a community and a place to live, they also ran a few "cottage industries" to support the community. I would be able to plug into these. At this point, I was amazed that anyone would want me and thankfully accepted their invitation.

For the first several hours, I experienced a huge sense of relief. God loved me! I was given a basement room. It wasn't ideal, but compared to where I had come from, it seemed like the "promised land." Besides, I now had to atone for the misdeeds of a lifetime. Even though God now loved me, years of rebellion couldn't be overlooked without consequence, but the consequence seemed to consist of the return of the terror several short hours after moving in. Perhaps the suffering would last only a little longer, and after I had made my atonement, I would then experience God's love?

My car was still in my possession. I resolved to keep it in good working order in the event that I could no longer bear the pain. I didn't want to die, but if staying alive would become utterly unendurable, I would have to call it quits. I'd make it seem like an accident. I'd plow my car into a big oak tree. I was already trying to pick one out.

There was no escape from the depression and terror. Sleep was shattered into minute-by-minute intervals. I could no longer put enough words together to constitute a passable prayer. Instead, prayer had become inchoate groans. I "slept" with the Bible in my arms, convinced that this was the most pious thing I could do.

I wanted to leave the community. I suspected that, in their eyes, I was doing penance for my years of rebellion. At least that's the way it felt. But I had become as immobile as my mule had been, and I wasn't sure from where I could derive the courage to make my move. One day, I ran into my old friend Charlie. Hearing selected portions of my tale of woe, he invited me to move in. I was moved the same day.

For years I struggled on, wanting desperately to believe that God loved me and was in my life, but finding that all the evidence was lining up on the other side. Looking to myself and my performance no longer sufficed to give me the assurance I longed for. If anything, it served to undermine what little hope I had. I had seen myself as God's partner, but because I hadn't been holding up my side of the partnership, I lost confidence that He would uphold His.

I desperately needed to rebuild and find renewed hope in God. I started to go to church with Charlie. Brother Dick was due in town to lead a revival. If anyone could diagnose the source of my grief, it was Brother Dick. He possessed every supernatural gift in the Book: discerning of spirits, prophecy, gifts of knowledge and healing. When Brother Dick came to town, everyone came to church. Charlie warned that we'd have to get there early.

Brother Dick didn't disappoint. He circumnavigated the church aisles, pointing to one and then to another with a word of prophecy. He told them about their businesses, their sins, but also about the triumphs that awaited them. The congregation was enthralled. Brother Dick was truly God's gift and intermediary. After his sermon, people spontaneously formed a line all around the church and even outside so that Brother Dick could pray for them individually. It was the pattern of this church for people to come up to the altar after the sermon to receive prayer from others who'd place their hands upon them. However, this was all suspended when Brother Dick was present. Everyone wanted to be prayed for directly by this man of God.

Charlie had graciously accompanied me in the line. Finally, it was my turn.

"I want you to pray that I'd receive the baptism of the Holy Spirit," I stated timidly. I didn't want to go into my experiences with depression and panic disorder. I had heard from many that once you receive the "baptism," you become so empowered by the presence of God, that hurts don't affect you the same way anymore. Receiving the "baptism" would minister to me across the spectrum of my needs and pains.

"And you're trying to say that you're saved?" brother Dick retorted in holy disbelief.

"I think I am. I've believed what the Bible's said about Jesus," I sheepishly responded, hoping that he would assent to my belief. If anyone knew with certainty that I was saved, it was Brother Dick.

"Am I hearing you right? Are you trying to tell me that you're saved?" he responded with even more incredulity. Perhaps I wasn't truly a believer, but I could answer only with the tiny amount of conviction that I had.

"I believe that I am," I pleaded.

"Then you're not living for the Lord, are you?" he fired back. By now, the entire church was looking on at this pretender who Brother Dick was exposing with all the wisdom that God had given him.

"I admit I'm not doing a good job of it, but I try," I responded, hoping he'd change his tune. Reluctantly, he began to pray for me to receive the "baptism," instructing me to say whatever came into my mouth. With an impatient wave of the hand, he directed me to step aside as he took on the next one in line.

Charlie, having been a witness to my pain and humiliation, beckoned me to sit down beside him.

"Danny, I know that his words were painful, but I'm sure that he didn't mean it the way it came out. He was probably thrown off by your depression. I'm sure that if you go back to Brother Dick after he's finished praying, he'll be able to say some things to make it right."

I wasn't as sure as Charlie. How could this man of God be so wrong? Perhaps he was right? In any event, it didn't seem as if I had a lot to lose, and we were finally standing before Brother Dick again.

"Brother Dick, why did you say what you did to me?" I asked in as humble a way as I possibly could.

"Do you know what you were praying?" he asked as if he was

sure that I knew.

"No, I just was saying whatever came into my mouth as you had told me to do." Had I been praying with the tongue of the devil? I thought.

"You're trying to tell me that you have no knowledge of what you were saying?" he continued as before, trying to pull the stubborn truth out of me.

"Not at all," I tried to reassure him.

Seeing my sincerity and confusion, he responded, "Don't worry about it. It's OK. Just get yourself into a good church, follow their program, and everything will be fine."

At this point, I had grave doubts about my ability to follow anyone's program, but what other choice did I have? God was my only hope, but I didn't seem to be able to avail myself of that hope. God was distant, and it seemed as if my best efforts wouldn't get me there. As much as I wanted to trust in this distant God, I had to first get there. Before I could luxuriate in His heavenly abode, the purity of my faith or the depth of my repentance or the sincerity of my love for Him had to transport me there. However, as I regarded the worthiness of these transports to get me there, I despaired. If it was up to me, I was lost.

Although I didn't realize it at the time, I needed a new hope. The hope I gradually came to was the hope of the Gospel of Grace. Yes, I had read about this hope for several years and even thought that I had been embracing this very hope. However, I didn't see it! As long as things were working reasonable well for me, I wouldn't see it. It was just too radical, too removed from the normal ways we see things. I had construed the Gospel in a manner that made human sense, in a truncated way. You reap what you sow—that was it! Christian salvation and growth were fundamentally up to us. God had opened his hand and had placed within reach everything we needed. Now it was up to us to make use of the disciplines and the blessings that God had made available.

However, through years of bitter struggle, I found that my own strength failed me; I was unable to sow. I wasn't even able to maintain my faith. In fact, I wasn't able to do anything of any real value (John 15:3-5), least of all manipulate God into loving me by virtue of my obedience.

Dying to our exaggerated opinions of self is incredibly painful and requires years, perhaps lifetimes. However, it is to the broken that God reveals Himself. Only the broken can eat from the 'tree of life' (Psalm 25:14). Those who trust in their own righteousness can't even see the Kingdom of God (John 3:3). Our delusions obscure the Kingdom from human sight.

What I'm talking about is a major overhaul, a humbling and a breaking down, which have to precede the glorification. It requires radical surgery followed by the right nourishment (1 Peter 2:2). Our thinking and attitudes have to undergo transformation (Rom 12:2). They're our chaperones to heaven's gate.

Our feelings are strongly influenced by the way we see and understand things. When I was a young and aspiring writer, I was in the market for offbeat experiences. I was convinced that these would serve as a deep reservoir from which I could draw materials for my writing. I would do dangerous things, things that others wouldn't do, to find these experiences. One night I was mugged at knifepoint. I was thrilled—some new grist for the mill. I had regarded this type of thing as a "positive." Another would have been traumatized.

We have to see God and ourselves correctly; we have to understand the Gospel as it truly is. The way we understand is the way we generally experience God. The way I understand my wife Anita is largely the way that I feel about her. If I was convinced that whenever I left our apartment, she would enjoy her various lovers in our building, this would affect the way I felt about her. However, if instead I was convinced that she was just looking for ways to please me, I would feel in an entirely different way towards her.

I say this because when we are engulfed in brokenness, the idea of changing our thinking seems so inadequate to address our hurting. We need a cannon blast not a feather, a new mind and not a new thought. Let me use another example: a friend of mine just won the "employee of the year" award. It had been a complete surprise, and he was elated. A mere change of perception gave him a profound lift. Of course you'll argue that this wasn't a mere change in perception but also in circumstance. This is true, but the change in circumstance wouldn't have done him any good had he not *known* about it. This is our circumstance! We are profoundly rich, loved, and protected, but we just don't see it. We have been invited to become rulers of the universe, to enjoy the most intimate love affair imaginable, but this reality fails to impact our hearts.

Paul tells us that we're immeasurably enriched when we come to the true knowledge of God.

> "For I want you to know what a great conflict I have for you... [2] that their hearts may be encouraged, being knit together in love, and *attaining* to all riches of the full assurance of understanding, to the knowledge of the mystery of God, both of the Father and of Christ, [3]in whom are hidden all the treasures of wisdom and knowledge." **Col. 2:1-3**

I found this so true for myself. As I grew in understanding of who God is and what His Gospel of grace is truly about, I gained a sense of freedom and confidence in Him. I came to see that it wasn't about me at all. I had been purchased, and I no longer belonged to myself. I was being carried in the loving arms of a God I was just beginning to learn about. No, I didn't entirely understand the events of my life or why I had to suffer to the degree that I did, but I began to understand that God had a purpose for all of it, a loving purpose that didn't depend upon whether or not my response was adequate enough.

This may seem very clinical or antiseptic to many of you who struggle with great pain and despair. It might seem to you that much more headier stuff is necessary to get you to turn the corner. We often think in terms of a 'mountain top' experience which will cut us free from our painful bonds. Moses had the ultimate mountain top experience. He had been with the Lord for 40 days and nights. When he came down to the people, his face glowed from being with the Lord. However, rather than telling the people about his experience or how they could have one for themselves, he instructed them in the teaching of God.

It's interesting to note what it was that caused Moses to glow.

We naturally think that by merely being in the presence of God, we'll be positively transformed, and therefore, if God would only draw near to us, we'd be changed for the better. It follows from this analysis that God is holding out on us, which is the very accusation of the Serpent (Gen. 3:5).

It wasn't the mere presence of God that caused Moses to glow, but instead the truth of God, which He was speaking to Moses.

> Now it was so, when Moses came down from Mount Sinai (and the two tablets of the Testimony *were* in Moses' hand when he came down from the mountain), that Moses did not know that the skin of his face shone *while he talked with Him.* **Exodus 34:29**

We have incorrect ideas about transformation. We place our hope in the wrong places. It is so difficult for us to see that what we believe has transformative power in the hand of the Spirit. It's easier to believe that if we only were able to change our brain chemistry, we could achieve the sought after transformation. (I'm not against the use of psychotropic medications, but I don't regard them as transformational.) In contrast, Jesus claimed that His followers were cleansed through His Word (John 15:3). Why should it be any different now?

This has been the uniform testimony of Scripture, that we are transformed and blessed through what we believe and understand. Of course, it is God Himself who molds us according to His will, but to do this, He uses the instrumentality of the Word. Paul tells us we're thoroughly equipped through the Word (2 Tim 3:16-17); Peter tells us that all the good things we receive come through the "knowledge of His Word" (2 Pet. 1:3-4).

How long does it take? It's a journey that ends with a divine encounter. It's only then that we'll be totally transformed, that we'll see ourselves in the image of God (1 John 3:2-3). I had received poor teaching. I think that with better, grace-centered teaching, I wouldn't have had to languish all the years that I did. However, God had a purpose for even that. The truths I learned, I learned the hard way, through the tears that melted them down into the crevices of my soul. As I despaired of self, seeing the total sufficiency of God put my fears to rest. As I despaired of my own righteousness, the gift of God's perfect righteousness became so unbelievably beautiful. As I lay suffocating in a pool of my own shame, God's glory and the promise of sharing it became so uplifting. I learned to rejoice in my own weaknesses and afflictions, because through them, I came to see God's beauty in 3-D. In short, it's all about Him, our shield against the ravages of sin, self-concern, and failure.

Daniel is available to come and speak on the topics raised in this book. He can be reached at (718) 237-0510 or at DANIEL@knowingscripture.com. You can also visit his website: knowingscripture.com

Daniel has been teaching Apologetics and Theology at the New York School of the Bible since 1992. You may call (212) 975-0170 ext. 23 to obtain a schedule of courses.

Printed in the United States
22894LVS00004B/61-510

9 781594 676949